T0007434

AN EMERGENCY IN
OTTAWA

AN EMERGENCY IN
OTTAWA

The Story of the Convoy Commission

PAUL WELLS

SQ

SUTHERLAND HOUSE

Sutherland House
416 Moore Ave., Suite 205
Toronto, ON M4G 1C9

First edition, April 2023

If you are interested in inviting one of our authors to a live event or media appearance, please contact sranasinghe@sutherlandhousebooks.com and visit our website at sutherlandhousebooks.com for more information about our authors and their schedules.

We acknowledge the support of the Government of Canada.

Manufactured in Canada
Cover designed by Lena Yang
Book composed by Karl Hunt

Library and Archives Canada Cataloguing in Publication
Title: An emergency in Ottawa : the story of the Convoy Commission / Paul Wells.
Other titles: Story of the Convoy Commission
Names: Wells, Paul A. (Paul Allen), author.
Description: Series statement: Sutherland quarterly | Includes bibliographical references.
Identifiers: Canadiana (print) 2023018992X | Canadiana (ebook) 20230190014 |
ISBN 9781990823251 (softcover) | ISBN 9781990823268 (EPUB)
Subjects: LCSH: Public Order Emergency Commission (Canada) |
LCSH: Canada. Emergencies Act. | LCSH: Freedom Convoy (2022 : Ottawa, Ont.) |
LCSH: Emergencies—Law and legislation—Canada. |
LCSH: Emergency management—Canada—Decision making.
Classification: LCC KE5460 .W45 2023 | DDC 342/.71062—dc23

ISBN 978-1-9908232-5-1
eBook 978-1-9908232-6-8

ABOUT THE AUTHOR

Paul Wells is one of Canada's most experienced political journalists. After many years at Maclean's, National Post and The Gazette, he now publishes a subscription newsletter at paulwells.substack.com. He is a frequent commentator on French-language and English-language radio and television.

Also by Paul Wells

Right Side Up: The Fall of Paul Martin and the Rise of Stephen Harper's New Conservatism

The Longer I'm Prime Minster: Stephen Harper and Canada, 2006-

To Alison Uncles

CONTENTS

INTRODUCTION

When I was a cub reporter in Montreal, I pulled a day's duty covering a coroner's inquest. An emergency response vehicle had run over a schoolchild out near Concordia University's Loyola campus in the city's west end. Covering the aftermath of that stupid tragedy was sad but fascinating work, as witnesses and lawyers retraced the doomed child's last crossing of Sherbrooke Street again and again.

I've never done serious time as a court reporter, but I've had the odd occasion to relive the feeling I had that day, of rules and procedure showing up late to make sense of chaos and grief. It's the job of lawyers to drain such events of drama, but they never quite manage it, do they? Lives have already been changed. Depending on the result of the lawyers' work, the laws might be left in such a state that more lives will be changed in the future.

On Valentine's Day, 2022, hundreds of trucks had been parked around Parliament Hill in Ottawa for seventeen days. Others had gathered around the Ambassador Bridge in Windsor, Ontario and at Coutts, Alberta for almost as long. Prime Minister Justin Trudeau had had enough, so he read a memo from his clerk of the Privy Council, paused to reflect, and signed it. This had the effect of declaring a "public order emergency" under the Emergencies Act, a federal statute that had never been used since it was passed by Parliament in 1988. Parliament would debate and the House of Commons would vote on the invocation of the act (Trudeau would revoke it before the Senate got a chance to vote). But under the terms of the act, Trudeau's signature was sufficient to bring it into effect.

Introduction

For a few days, not much seemed to happen. Then, early in the morning of February 18, the Ottawa Police Service, working effectively at last with the Ontario Provincial Police and the Royal Canadian Mounted Police, told protesters through loudspeakers that it was time to leave or face arrest. Exit lanes on surrounding streets were kept open. Few of the protesters took them. Police cleared sections of street near Parliament Hill until 8 p.m., then paused for the night in front of the Château Laurier hotel. The next morning, they went back to work and finished clearing the downtown core. On February 20, they cleared a secondary logistics hub a few kilometres east of Parliament Hill.

"Between February 18 and 20," Justice Paul Rouleau would write in the 2,000-page report of his commission of inquiry into the first-ever use of the Emergencies Act, "police in Ottawa made 273 arrests and laid 422 charges. More broadly, between January 28 and March 31, 2022, the Ottawa Police Service laid 533 criminal charges against 140 individuals for actions arising from the Freedom Convoy. Police towed or impounded 110 vehicles." Significantly, Rouleau added: "No charges were laid under the Emergency Measures Regulations."

Some 280 accounts worth about $8 million were frozen. Fewer than 280 people were affected because some had more than one account. The RCMP told financial institutions on February 21, a week after the act came into force, that it no longer considered anyone's accounts worth freezing.

The Emergencies Act itself requires that a public inquiry be held each time it is used. Trudeau knew when he signed the Clerk's memo that a judge would be calling witnesses to argue about whether he'd done the right thing. And more than one judge: the act's preamble states that any government using it would remain "subject to the Canadian Charter of Rights and Freedoms and the Canadian Bill of Rights," so court challenges independent of the commission of inquiry were also inevitable.

The Emergencies Act is a product of a particular moment. It was passed by the government of Brian Mulroney, a Progressive Conservative whose political mission was in part to atone for the excesses of Pierre Trudeau, especially in Quebec, where both men had built successive and competitive bases of power. Trudeau was the last prime minister to use the War Measures Act, which had been written and used for real wars, in the context of some terrorist kidnappings in Montreal in 1970 that, whatever they were, weren't a war. Mulroney wanted to trim the excesses of the War Measures Act, to tuck its provisions under those of a Charter of Rights that didn't exist in 1970. He handed the task to his young defence minister, Perrin Beatty. John Turner, who had been justice minister during the 1970 crisis and was now leader of the official opposition, watched and decided to help. The Liberals and New Democrats proposed dozens of amendments. Beatty implemented most of them. It was a time when the phrase "act of Parliament" more often meant what it said than it does these days.

That long-ago Parliament left a smaller law for smaller crises. Here is a small book about what happened next. The larger book has already been written by Paul Rouleau, running to five volumes and 2,000 pages. His is definitive. But he left some room to contemplate what happens when absolutely everyone in Canada is exhausted after two years of sickness, death and politics, and a government and the citizens who hate it most get into a shoving match.

Hard cases make for bad law, as lawyers like to say. I don't know about that, but they usually make for a hell of a story.

CHAPTER 1

A SUDDEN SEASON

One of the first things I noticed about the room where Paul Rouleau was hearing testimony about the first-ever use of the Emergencies Act was that by the middle of November, it was a petri dish of low-grade infection.

For all I knew, the scratchy throats and red eyes might have been going on for a few days before I noticed them. These things can sneak up on you. But on November 14, while Shantona Chaudhury, the co-lead counsel for the Rouleau Commission, was putting questions to Robert Stewart, who for a while had been deputy minister of Public Safety in the Government of Canada, I noticed Chaudhury had a cough.

A commission of inquiry is like a trial, but not really. Paul Rouleau, the government-appointed commissioner, had recruited a team of lawyers with sterling reputations who would take turns questioning witnesses on his behalf. They were helpers more than grand inquisitors, coaxing rather than confronting. For this gentle task they were probably overqualified.

Chaudhury is a founding partner at Pape Chaudhury, a boutique Toronto civil-litigation firm with an outsized reputation. She graduated from Queen's University with a master's degree in French. She followed that with law school to "do something a bit more practical," as she later told the McGill law school magazine. At McGill, she helped found the law faculty's theatre troupe, Actus Reus. It's Latin for "the guilty act." She clerked for Ian Binnie at the Supreme Court of Canada. She's often returned to the top court to argue cases. And with that brief biographical sketch I've given you more of a glimpse into Chaudhury's complexity and humanity than any of us got to see during the six weeks of hearings of the Public Order Emergency Commission.

Once upon a time, you could build quite a reputation for yourself at a commission of inquiry. Make a name, put some quirks on display, get people talking about your career prospects. There once were days of startling revelations, cat-and-mouse interrogations, devil-may-care lawyering. The gold standard in this regard was the 1974 Cliche Commission into union raiding in the Quebec construction industry, when it seemed an entire generation of legal and political talent had come of age just in time to save Quebec from the worst excesses of the Quiet Revolution. Brian Mulroney! Lucien Bouchard! Guy Chevrette! Scrappy musketeers of truth and justice. Beefy heartthrobs in plaid sport coats and mutton-chop sideburns. Those were the days. They're gone now.

This latest thing was no showcase for legal peacocks. The Rouleau Commission was about a drama, but it wasn't drama. Sure, Brendan Miller, the lawyer for some of the Freedom Convoy organizers, managed to get himself kicked out of the room by Rouleau near the end, but it took strenuous effort and the overall effect was that Miller had miscast himself in someone else's courtroom.

Here there was too much work to do and too little time. Under terms written into the Emergencies Act itself, the government must appoint a commission of inquiry each time the act is put into force. And it mustn't dawdle. The commissioner has less than a year from his appointment to produce a final report. That's in the act, too.

To make matters even more hectic, the fates had cancelled what were supposed to be the first six weeks of the commission's public hearings.

The commissioner in charge of this inquiry was Justice Paul Rouleau of the Court of Appeal for Ontario. Taciturn, poker-faced, courteous to everyone in his hearing room, and not, it would appear, altogether well. Just before testimony was set to begin, the commission sent out a news release saying Rouleau needed surgery "to address a health issue that has very recently arisen." No further detail was offered. By mid-November, Rouleau was feeling much better, thanks for asking, but everyone around him was under the gun. Rouleau now had half the time he'd originally scheduled to hear more than sixty witnesses. The days would be long, the breaks brief, and, since Library and Archives Canada wouldn't be located in Ottawa's fine-dining district even if Ottawa had one, the lunches shitty. The commission's legal team had divided its titanic workload among them and done piles of preliminary interviews with witnesses, the better to make it through these six weeks of testimony with sanity nearly intact.

Chaudhury's co-lead counsel was Jeffrey Leon, two decades her senior, a natty dresser with a freshly grown and perhaps ill-considered lockdown goatee. Edmonton-born, a graduate of University of Toronto law school, Leon was co-head of litigation at Bennett Jones. It didn't matter to him that this was no place to make a reputation. His reputation was made. He was Jeff Leon. Bennett Jones started in Calgary in 1922, founded by R. B. Bennett before he became prime minister of Canada. But today Bennett Jones is everywhere, like God. From its empyrean suite on the thirty-fourth floor of One First Canadian Place in Toronto, where Leon works, you can almost see the northern tip of Baffin Island, where he met his wife Carol Best when they both ran a marathon, long ago, as close as a marathon runner could get to the North Pole. And, again, I've made Leon sound more interesting than Paul Rouleau ever did.

Under Chaudhury and Leon there were six senior counsel and twelve counsel, impeccable in background, sterling in accomplishment, interchangeable in manner. Since each of them had developed specific expertise in weeks of frantic prep sessions during Rouleau's convalescence, any one of them might be up at the front of the Winifred Bambrick Room on any given day, guiding a witness through the events of late January and early February, when crowds of protesters parking tonnes of rolling steel had occupied the central district of the capital city of what remains, at least technically, a G-7 country.

None of the proceedings in Rouleau's commission room came close to matching the outsized passions that had played out while the convoy held downtown Ottawa, and smaller copycat protests had paralyzed parts of Windsor, Ontario and Coutts, Alberta. The Rouleau Commission was about chaos sifted through process.

Probably the least important thing about all of this is Shantona Chaudhury's cough.

I want to emphasize that at no point did this cough seem like a big deal. It just wasn't in any hurry to go away. Since Chaudhury's work required her to talk, she tried various tactics for minimizing the effect of the cough. Sometimes she'd ball up a fist and cover her mouth in mid-sentence. Other times she'd do her best to ignore the tickle in her throat, hurrying to get to the end of a sentence but barking out an apologetic little cough before she could quite make it.

During breaks in the testimony, lawyers and witnesses would leave the Bambrick Room to mill, confer, or check their phones. A bunch of reporters would pour out of our workspace in the Margaret Avison Room, across the hall, to intercept and chat with them.

Let me tell you about the room names. Every room at Library and Archives Canada is named after a writer, in a rough inverse-proportion relation between the size of the room and the notoriety of the author. Mordecai Richler gets a conference room that fits only fifteen people. Winifred Bambrick, eponym of the Rouleau Commission's main hearing room, was a bit of a sensation as a harp player before the First World War. She recorded for Thomas Edison, whose ledger called her a "Canadian Child Harpist." Slander. She was twenty-two. In 1946, she won the Governor General's Award for her only novel, *Continental Revue*.

Margaret Avison, whose spirit watched over us in the slightly smaller press room, worked odd bookish jobs such as file clerk and librarian to support her poetry writing, which won her two Governor General's Awards. Her last collection opens: "A sudden season/ has changed our world./ Everybody is out/ to see, or bask, or/ with their kind to exuberate./ Everything is new." In the months after a plague and a siege, this sounded about right.

In the brief mingling intermissions between Rouleau commission witnesses, I caught up a few times with an old acquaintance who served as counsel for a group with standing in the inquiry. We would pause to gossip and trade analyses. When my lawyer friend talked, I heard an over-the-counter cough drop rattling around his back teeth, click-click-click. This, too, was no big deal. There were about forty people in a room for long days for weeks on end. A scratchy throat gets around. Two weeks later, when Justin Trudeau became the commission's last witness, it was Chaudhury who quizzed him. She still had her cough.

The cough and the cough drops stuck in the back of my mind because on the day I noticed them, November 14, Ontario's chief medical officer of health, Dr. Kieran Moore, held a news conference in Toronto to urge everyone to wear masks again in public. Emergency rooms were beyond capacity, he said. COVID, the seasonal flu, and a normally innocuous respiratory illness were tag-teaming the unprepared. Small children made up a disproportionate share of the caseload. They were filling emergency rooms past capacity. This "triple threat," Moore said, "requires our collective action" to "ensure that our health-care system remains able to care for Ontarians when they need it."

Moore was precisely the sort of figure whose counsel had carried great weight with most of the public for two years. Rightly so, if you ask me. Now, once again, he was pleading with us to wear masks. Any fool could see why. Yet almost nobody was listening. There might have been 100 people at a time in Library and Archives Canada, if you added the commission room, the press room, security, support staff, and a few TV camera guys at a scrum station near the exit door to Wellington Street. Out of the hundred, maybe three would have masks on at any given time.

Again, it's a little thing. By now almost everyone was vaccinated against COVID-19, including many in the little knot of convoy protesters who attended every day of the hearings. Most of us had also had our own tidy post-vaxx personal bout with COVID, a few days of feeling lousy with its backhanded parting gift of another layer of partial immunity. The likelihood of getting seriously sick from hanging around Library and Archives Canada without a mask was very low.

But this is something I couldn't help noticing about the Rouleau commission. By the time everyone sat down for six weeks of testimony, the deep social fracture that had given rise to the Freedom Convoy had gone dormant again. A few months before the trucks descended on Ottawa and Windsor and Coutts, the anti-COVID public-health restrictions in place were too fragmentary to galvanize any kind of wild, intense backlash. And a few months after the trucks left, governments had dismantled the rules requiring masks and proof of vaccination, on planes and trains, in concert halls and restaurants and in the federal public service. So we could all live together again. Not in perfect harmony, but at least with some minimal level of civility.

One of the challenges facing Paul Rouleau and the shifting casts that attended his court, then, was to remember how angry and exhausted everyone was when the convoy happened. To remember how poorly any of the protagonists understood the others' motives or intent. The hardest thing, when you know how the story ends, is to remember what it felt like not to know how it would end.

Having started in the middle, let me back up to the beginning. Friday, October 13, the first day of the commission's public hearings, was devoted to awkward introductions. Rouleau sat at the front of the Bambrick Room, behind a desk, off to one side. A second desk with chairs for a witness or two was stationed off to the other side, facing Rouleau. Watching the commissioner and the witnesses in a few tidy rows of chairs were the lawyers, first the commission's own, and then the lawyers representing the various parties that had standing in the proceedings. After that, a few more rows of seats for ordinary spectators, really anyone who wanted to show up on a given day and listen.

The last few rows near the exit door were originally reserved for reporters. There were not nearly enough seats for all the journalists assigned to cover the commission. Rouleau's media staff improvised lotteries to decide who would get which seats for the first three days. Then the first day's reporters filed into the room and discovered there were no desks on which we could perch laptop computers to write while everyone talked.

There were, however, such wonders across the hall in the Avison Room. We could watch the proceedings on a big video screen, hear simultaneous translation through headphones if needed, and take screen shots of assorted pieces of evidence as witnesses discussed them. We could even gossip, trade snarky remarks, and share a wide assortment of sweet and savoury snacks, whose most faithful purveyors were the reporters from the *National Post* and the *Toronto Star*. So after the first day, hardly any reporter wasted any time in the actual commission room. Across the hall, with our kind, we exuberated.

Rouleau opened by reading prepared remarks that amounted to a civics lesson. "Commissions of inquiry perform two important functions," he said. "They make findings of fact, and they make recommendations for the future." What happened, and what should happen next. So far, so general.

But then Rouleau discussed the specific mandate of his own commission and he began to drop important hints about how he saw his role. This had become an important question on the day Justin Trudeau's government appointed Rouleau to head the commission and published the order-in-council describing his mandate. Both the name of the commissioner and the details of his mandate led some observers to suspect Trudeau was tailoring the commission to his advantage.

Rouleau used to be an active Liberal. He worked on John Turner's leadership campaign in 1983 and served as a senior staffer in Turner's office. And his mandate was broad. The Emergencies Act itself calls for a commission of inquiry into "the circumstances that led to the declaration being issued and the measures taken for dealing with the emergency." But the Trudeau cabinet handed Rouleau a greatly expanded mandate to consider a long list of questions not mentioned in the act. Rouleau was told to consider the "evolution and goals of the convoy and blockades, their leadership, organization and participants;" the "impact of domestic and foreign funding, including crowdsourcing platforms;" the "impact, role and sources of misinformation and disinformation, including the use of social media;" the "impact of the blockades, including their economic impact;" and the "efforts of police and other responders prior to and after the declaration."

What these new additional mandates had in common was that they represented the actions of people who weren't the federal government. Whereas the mandates written into the law itself were about the federal government's own choices. So it was hardly surprising that some people suspected Trudeau was sending Rouleau on a wild goose chase. "The hope in [the Prime Minister's Office] is that politicians will get a pass from Rouleau," *Sun* newspaper columnist Brian Lilley wrote on the spring day Rouleau's mandate was announced.

But now the hearings were underway and Rouleau had the chance to speak for himself. He made it clear he was aware of the concerns about a too-broad mandate and eager to reassure listeners. "Unlike other commissions of inquiry, we have two mandates," he said. "One given to us by Parliament, and one given to us by Cabinet."

The mandate from Parliament "is found in the Emergencies Act itself," he said. Here he quoted the bit about "the circumstances" and "the measures." "The mandate from Parliament, therefore, is one of public accountability: the public's legitimate right to know why the government proclaimed an emergency, and whether the actions it took were appropriate."

In Rouleau's mind, this was clearly his most important task. It came from all of Parliament. The "additional mandate" came only from the smaller group of MPs who formed the Cabinet. This was the stuff about the blockade leadership, crowdfunding, and social media. And this additional mandate came with what Rouleau called "an important caveat:" he was to examine these second-tier topics only "to the extent relevant to the circumstances of the declaration and measures taken."

"In other words, although these topics have been identified as worthy of attention, it is the mandate that has been given to us by Parliament that drives the Commission's work," Rouleau said. "While this inquiry will deal with a wide range of issues, its focus will remain squarely on the decision of the Federal Government."

With that, the commissioner wrapped up his civics lesson. Lawyers for each of the parties to whom Rouleau had granted standing took turns making brief remarks. These included residents of Ottawa who had seen their streets occupied; the municipal governments of Ottawa, Windsor, and Coutts; the police forces of Ottawa, Ontario, and the nation; the convoy protesters themselves; and groups that worry enough about civil rights in the abstract to defend them in the particular.

Shantona Chaudhury, the commission co-lead counsel, gave the best look ahead. The more than sixty witnesses—in the end there would be seventy-six, after some were added and Ontario Premier Doug Ford ran like a barnyard chicken—would not be heard scattershot, but in thematic groupings, she said. The first to testify would be the people of Ottawa, some of their merchants, and their municipal government. Then the police, municipal and provincial. Then several key figures from the Freedom Convoy itself. After hearing from witnesses who dealt with local variations of the convoy mess, in Windsor and Coutts, the hearings would wind down with a very long list of federal government officials, cabinet ministers, their staffers, and the RCMP. Justin Trudeau would close the festivities.

I have borrowed this order for what follows. Successive chapters of this little book will treat the testimony and experiences of the capital, the police, the protesters, and Team Trudeau. Again, I have no interest in being comprehensive. This is my tour of highlights, background, and paths left unexplored. It's a study of decision-making in a catastrophe, a look at the workings of an anthill when some mischievous god is frying the ants with a magnifying glass while they work.

We begin with a virus in Wuhan.

CHAPTER 2

WHERE WE BEGAN

A couple of weeks before Christmas 2019 in Wuhan, a city of 10 million in the central Chinese province of Hubei, people started to experience pneumonia-like symptoms that didn't respond well to the usual treatments. By New Year's Eve, there were fifty-nine suspected cases. By January 22, 2020, the new disease had killed six people and Chinese public-health officials had published the genetic sequence of the tiny culprit, a "novel coronavirus," or new strain of a familiar family of viruses. At the end of January, a total of 9,962 cases were confirmed across China.

The disease soon spread to other countries. The World Health Organization reported COVID-19 cases in twenty by the end of January and fifty-four a month after that.

A man in Toronto who had been visiting Wuhan became Canada's first confirmed case on January 23. His wife became the second. They both recovered. The disease progressed slowly in Canada, at first. British Columbia reported its first case on January 27, Quebec not for another month. But on March 5, a staffer at the Lynn Valley Care Centre in North Vancouver tested positive for COVID-19. She hadn't been travelling. "Community spread" had come to Canada. Three days later, a resident at Lynn Valley, a man in his eighties with a batch of pre-existing conditions, became the first Canadian to die with COVID-19.

By the end of March, sixty-six people with COVID had died in Canada. It was clear this new virus was a serious problem. It remained only to see how serious.

On January 30, the director-general of the World Health organization declared a Public Health Emergency of International Concern (PHEIC). This is the WHO's formal method for flagging outbreaks that deserve international attention and prompt reporting.

It was the WHO's sixth PHEIC since 2009, including that year's H1N1 flu outbreak and two subsequent Ebola outbreaks. Which means that the declaration of an emergency, in itself, didn't give individuals or even their governments a lot of specific information about what to think. During a PHEIC, WHO members (most of the countries in the world, including Canada) are required to report local outbreaks and inform the public that a health threat is likely to cross national borders.

A few borders? All of them? It depends. Many countries were affected only slightly, if at all, by several of the WHO's earlier emergencies. At first, WHO didn't sound particularly fussed. Four days after declaring the emergency, its executive board was told there was no need for measures that "unnecessarily interfere with international travel and trade." The international spread of the virus was "minimal and slow."

Politicians elsewhere partook in the same general passivity. In a relaxed, jokey scrum with reporters on March 10, Patty Hajdu, the federal health minister, twice sought to "remind" Canadians "that right now the risk is low."

By then, the WHO was changing its mind. March 11, it declared COVID-19 a pandemic. There's actually no provision in the WHO's International Health Regulations dealing with "pandemics." By itself, the new label changed nothing about the mechanics of the international response to the virus. Essentially, all WHO had done was find a scarier word than "emergency." But tone matters. On March 13, Quebec declared a public-health emergency. Justin Trudeau, whose wife Sophie had been diagnosed with COVID after attending a WE Day event in London with Idris Elba, cancelled a meeting with the premiers that had been planned for the same day. Alone in their homes, Canadians pondered the gravity of this strange new situation.

On Wednesday, March 18, Trudeau's government banned most air travel into Canada. The following weekend, the Canada-US border was closed to non-essential land traffic for the first time in history.

Governments everywhere tried to juggle the competing claims of safety, commerce, and society. At first, safety won big. Staying safe was easy. A virus is a simple thing that follows simple rules. It can't reproduce without a host, so it can't hurt anyone it can't reach. The more space people kept between them, the fewer chances the virus would find new hosts.

Society and commerce responded: *Okay, but we can't keep this up forever.* People wanted to gather. Businesses needed to operate. How long would everyone have to avoid everyone else?

We've actually never shut down our civilization for a couple of years before. At first, almost nobody thought we'd need to. It's easy to forget that a lot of early predictions, based on nothing, were wildly optimistic. I've bookmarked a Reuters story from the second week of the lockdown that seemed depressingly glum at the time. It reported that at a virtual town-hall meeting for Pentagon staffers, the US defence secretary, Mike Esper, said: "I think we need to plan for this to be a few months long at least."

"Late May, June, something in that range. Could be as late as July," concurred Mark Milley, the chairman of the Joint Chiefs of Staff.

July gave way to September 2020. Then to 2021. Inevitably, public-health measures see-sawed over time between social distance and permissiveness. In Canada, the balance varied from province to province, sometimes from urban settings to rural, and as the rules changed, they became almost impossible to keep straight.

Alberta Premier Jason Kenney banned gatherings of more than fifty people, indoors or out, on March 17. Ten days later, he lowered the maximum permitted crowd size to fifteen. In mid-May, the limit went back up to fifty for outdoor gatherings but stayed at fifteen for indoor gatherings. Then on June 12, as warm weather seemed to reduce the number of infections, Alberta eliminated crowd caps altogether. This had the entirely predictable effect of making infection rates rise again. At the end of October, Kenney's government capped gatherings again at fifteen. But only in Edmonton and Calgary.

Between March and June, Saskatchewan's limit on indoor crowds bounced from twenty-five to ten, then back up to fifteen, then up again to thirty. The larger numbers were an expression of hope springing eternal. Autumn brought disappointment: the crowd limit tightened back to fifteen, to ten, and to five as the days grew shorter. Finally, just before Christmas, Scott Moe's government banned indoor gatherings altogether. Those are just the rule changes for 2020. There would be two more years of this.

Every time they tweaked the rules, politicians everywhere swore they were following the science. For part of 2021, Ontario had a "Stay-at-Home Order" that listed twenty-nine approved exceptions. Quebec, next door, had a curfew after 8 p.m., with eleven approved exceptions. So Quebec was more permissive during the day and less at night.

The Rouleau Commission's "overview report" summarizing various governments' reaction to the virus points out that Doug Ford's Ontario government issued over 200 orders-in-council in respect of the pandemic in 2020 alone. This is a perfectly asinine level of information to dump on any citizenry. Ford's only excuse is that everyone was doing it. In a bit of theatre that soon came to play like grim satire, each province's premier would stand next to a grim-looking scientist in a lab coat when announcing the latest rule changes. Somewhere in all this, spotting a permissiveness gradient that would last who knew how long, I hurried from Ottawa to Montreal for a haircut that was permitted in only the latter city.

Different people responded to the restrictions in different ways. For the longest time, most people were reasonably happy to obey the assorted public-health orders. Some really weren't. On April 25, barely a month into the global lockdown, about 100 people protested at Queen's Park in front of Ontario's legislature. The next day, fifty people marched through Vancouver's West End. Four days after that, 200 in

Edmonton. A convoy of vehicles drove around the Alberta legislature, honking horns, the *Edmonton Journal* noted.

On it went. More than 300 protesters were back at Queen's Park on May 2. Seventy outside the Manitoba legislature a week after that. Protest planners grew more ambitious. On July 19, coordinated "March to Unmask" protests took place in Vancouver, Calgary, Saskatoon, Winnipeg, and Ottawa. Montreal fielded a really big crowd, numbering in the thousands, on August 8. At the end of that month, hundreds gathered on Parliament Hill in Ottawa.

Later, it would be fashionable in some circles to wonder what on earth had provoked these protests and to assume the answer must be "Americans." But anti-lockdown protests were a global phenomenon from the outset or, rather, they were a local phenomenon everywhere. The Carnegie Endowment for International Peace has operated an online Global Protest Tracker since 2017. Its log of COVID-related protests begins as soon as lockdowns started. The first countries Carnegie lists as venues for such protests are Brazil, Columbia, Israel, Italy, Lebanon, Slovenia and Argentina.

On the last Saturday in August 2020, the same day Ottawa saw its first sizable anti-lockdown protests, thousands marched in London, England and tens of thousands in Berlin. Most of the German protesters were peaceful. A few got ideas and tried to storm the Reichstag, Germany's parliament. Police in riot gear blocked the way. Later, after the January 6, 2021 attack by sore losers on the Capitol building in Washington, and after the Freedom Convoy occupation of Ottawa, footage from the 2020 Reichstag attack would look terribly familiar.

It is nevertheless true that the early reaction against COVID restrictions was more visceral and theatrical in parts of the United States than in much of the rest of the world. Part of this is down to the presidency of Donald J. Trump, whose entire tenure in office was a kind of generalized licence to his admirers to lose their shit when they felt like it. But elements of the early reaction to COVID restrictions in the US Midwest read today as uncanny foreshadowing of events in Ottawa, Windsor, and Coutts nearly two years later.

Luke Mogelson's book *The Storm is Here: An American Crucible* is a diary of civil unrest in the United States from 2020 to 2022. Events gave Mogelson a lot of material, but he begins in Michigan. "On April 15, 2020, thousands of vehicles convoyed to Lansing and clogged the streets surrounding the state capital for a protest that had been advertised as 'Operation Gridlock.' Signs warned of revolt. Someone waved an upside-down American flag. Already—nine months before January 6, seven months before the election, six weeks before a national uprising for police accountability and racial justice—there were a lot of them and they were mad."

Mogelson writes that Operation Gridlock spurred copycat protests in more than thirty states. "In Kentucky, the governor was hanged in effigy outside the capitol; in North Carolina, a protester hauled a rocket launcher through downtown Raleigh; in California, a journalist covering an anti-lockdown demonstration was held at knifepoint; ahead of a rally in Salt Lake City, a man wrote on Facebook, 'Bring your guns, the civil war starts Saturday . . . The time is now.'"

Canada is distinct from the United States to this extent at least: organized and large-scale protest against government COVID restrictions started much later here. Although, come to think of it, it depends where you start counting. The Rouleau Commission's "Overview Report: Early Protest Activities and Legal Challenges Relating to Public Health Measures" begins its list of protests with a high-profile incident more than a year before COVID hit Canada.

"On February 14, 2019, a convoy of trucks known as 'United We Roll' left Red Deer, Alberta, bound for Ottawa to protest the federal government's energy policies," the commission's report says. "CBC reported that around 170 trucks of varying sizes left Red Deer as part of the convoy. Arriving in Ottawa on February 19, 2019, United We Roll participated in two days of demonstrations on and around Parliament Hill before dispersing."

United We Roll also took some inspiration from events abroad, especially the Yellow Vest protests in France in 2018. All of these movements around the world feed on one another. United We Roll's stated motives were a grab bag. "Pipelines need to be built. Bill C-69 and 48 are obviously a problem," United We Roll organizer Jason Corbeil told the Ottawa Citizen. C-69 was a substantial reinforcement of environmental assessment of major infrastructure projects. In Alberta, it's sometimes known as the "No More Pipelines Act." C-48 is a ban on oil tanker traffic off the British Columbia coast. "And (so is) the carbon tax. We're about to show a country that we can unite and stand together against a government that isn't listening to us."

United We Roll's truckers gathered on and around Parliament Hill overnight, then dispersed. While they were clustered on Wellington Street in front of the Centre Block, Conservative Party leader Andrew Scheer spoke to the crowd. Later and some distance away, Faith Goldy, a right-wing social-media star, climbed onto a truck-mounted platform. She led the crowd in a chant of "Commie scum off our streets/ Commie scum off our streets." (Nobody puts real effort into coming up with good slogans any more.) "No more Trudeau," she added. "Our borders will be protected against illegal immigrants!"

On Canada Day, 2020, three and a half months into the COVID lockdown, a smaller protest group, calling itself Canadian Revolution, rallied on Parliament Hill and then set up a tent city on a patch of grass next to the Canadian War Memorial.

On the same Canada Day, another man arrived in Ottawa, travelling alone. Corey Hurren was a master corporal with the Canadian Rangers. He ran a small sausage-making company outside Bowsman, Manitoba. Life for Hurren had become an accumulation of woe. He couldn't sell enough sausage to cover his small-business loan. The Lion's Club where he volunteered shut down when COVID hit. The Rangers throttled back their activity, too. When Hurren sought to renew his firearms license, he was told new gun laws had made some of the weapons he inherited from his father illegal. There are places in this country where people feel they only ever hear from government when it tells them to stop doing something they thought was fine.

Hurren packed his father's firearms into his pickup truck, which the dealer was planning to repossess because Hurren couldn't make payments. He drove to Ottawa, wrote an apologetic note to his family sharing his fear that Canada "is now under a communist dictatorship," and rammed the gate at Rideau Hall. Justin Trudeau was living in a secondary residence on the Rideau Hall grounds because he couldn't make up his mind about repairs to the official residence at 24 Sussex Drive. On this particular day, he wasn't home.

Once he'd burst through the gate, Hurren climbed down from his truck and walked around for a few minutes with some of his guns. He didn't really have a plan. He assumed the police would shoot him dead. He was arrested, tried, and convicted to six years on mischief and firearms charges.

Better timing and a bit more pep would have made Hurren a mortal threat to a sitting prime minister. As was Michael Zehaf-Bibeau when he opened fire outside Stephen Harper's Conservative caucus room in 2014. Or André Dallaire, who hopped a fence and made it as far as the bedroom where Jean and Aline Chrétien slept, days after the 1995 Quebec referendum. Three of the last four Canadian prime ministers have faced real threats that we know of. But the guy who made it to Trudeau's lawn had a truck and a grudge about COVID. Which meant that anytime ever after that trucks and COVID got mentioned in the same breath, Trudeau's briefings would include a reference to Corey Hurren.

The arrival of working vaccines made Canada's national patchwork of COVID rules more complex. Health Canada approved the first mRNA vaccine, from Pfizer-BioNTech, on December 9, 2020. Moderna's candidate won authorization two weeks after that. For the first half of 2021, demand for the new drugs far outstripped supply. While that lasted, anyone who didn't want a shot was almost a blessing, because their ambivalence meant a shorter line for people who did.

But by mid-2021, most people who wanted to be vaccinated had had their first dose. Growing numbers had two. Attention shifted to the ones who didn't want any. If governments could coerce social distancing, opening hours, and crowd limits, could they coerce vaccination as well?

"I'm really worried about that," Justin Trudeau replied, when YouTuber Brandon Gonez asked him about vaccine mandates on May 9, 2021. Telling people they couldn't go to a concert or a sporting event without being vaccinated might be a great "motivator," the prime minister said. But "what do you do with someone . . . who for religious or deep convictions decides that, no, they're not going to get a vaccine?"

What indeed? "We're not a country that makes vaccination mandatory," Trudeau said.

And you know what? Depending how you define these things, that never changed. There was never a federal law requiring vaccination against COVID-19. Just an ever-growing number of federal and provincial regulations listing places you couldn't go if you couldn't prove you were vaccinated. Commercial flights, VIA trains, and the federal public service first among them. "Consequences," as Trudeau called the measures during the late-summer federal election campaign.

It wouldn't be fair to call the Trudeau Liberals' new position a complete 180-degree reversal. But in direction and tone it was a sharp swerve from free choice toward constraint. What drove it? Probably some mix of genuine concern for public health and a keen understanding that opposition to vaccine mandates was highest among people who mistrusted government in general. Which is to say, among Trudeau's Conservative opponents.

Just as Canada's protesters had drawn inspiration from abroad, so now did the Trudeau Liberals. It was France's president, Emmanuel Macron, who in a nationally televised speech on July 12, 2021 set the example for governments that wanted to make it harder for their citizens to stay unvaccinated. Effective almost immediately, Macron said, "to get into a show, a theme park, a concert or a festival you must be vaccinated or show a recent negative test." By the beginning of August, vaccine passports would be required for entry into cafés, restaurants, shopping malls, planes, trains, and buses. "Everywhere, we will have the same guiding principle," Macron said. "Recognizing civic-mindedness and targeting restrictions at the unvaccinated rather than on everyone."

Macron's message was clear: getting vaccinated would give you options that wouldn't be available to the unvaccinated.

A few days after his televised speech, stronger quotes attributed to Macron circulated on Facebook. "I no longer have any intention of sacrificing my life, my time, my freedom and the adolescence of my daughters, as well as their right to study properly, for those who refuse to be vaccinated. This time you stay at home, not us."

The widely-circulated quote was made up, fake news. But it felt great to read, if you were inclined to believe, as many Canadians were, that the main obstacles to ending confinement and a resumption of freedom were these throwbacks who refused to get their shots. We were so close. A bit of pushing was all the holdouts needed.

And as one veteran Liberal strategist pointed out, it could also help Justin Trudeau win an election.

On August 11, 2021, the *Globe and Mail* carried an op-ed article by Peter Donolo, Jean Chrétien's old communications director. He's still an active Liberal, not overly impressed with the Trudeau crew, but willing to give it occasional advice. "Vaccine passports could win Trudeau a majority," the headline on Donolo's article read.

Mandatory vaccination was the right thing to do, Donolo wrote. "Until we have a nationwide, coast-to-coast standard to safeguard Canadians from infection spread by those who refuse to be inoculated, our chain of protection will be as strong as its weakest link." But requiring vaccination was also good politics. A huge majority of Canadians already had at least one dose of vaccine. "Anyone who has ever advised a political leader will tell you that when you have an issue that roughly 80 per cent of the electorate agree on, you have a winner," Donolo wrote. "Especially if your main opponent won't touch it."

I've chatted with Peter Donolo since 2021. He doesn't like it when I point out that Trudeau got the governor general to kick off the 2021 election four days after Donolo's article ran, and that a plan for federal recognition of provincial vaccine passports was Liberal policy in that election. Donolo thinks I overstate his influence. But to me, saying the Donolo op-ed and the Liberal platform are connected is like saying the Michigan protests of 2020 and the Freedom Convoy of 2022 are connected. Perhaps there was no causal link. There's just a community of thought.

Standing in front of Rideau Hall, the prime minister said he needed a new mandate to guide Canadians through the peril's next hours. "I don't accept any party saying we shouldn't do everything we can to keep people safe and to end this pandemic and rebuild," he said. "And I certainly don't accept any politician saying you shouldn't have your choice on how to do that or on what comes next."

Canadians chose, after a fashion. Trudeau's re-elected Liberals implemented their promises. Starting on October 30, passengers on Canadian flights and trains had to show proof of vaccination or a negative PCR test result. A month later, the PCR test was no longer good enough. Only vaccination would suffice.

In a bunch of federally regulated sectors, the effective deadline for tightening restrictions was November 15. That was the date by which members of the Canadian Armed Forced needed to provide proof of vaccination. The same went for contractors who needed access to federal government workplaces; anyone working in federally regulated airlines and airports; and operators of most ships in Canadian waters.

The next day, on November 16, a truck driver from Wallaceburg, Ontario named Brigitte Belton was stopped by the Canadian Border Services Agency at the Windsor-Detroit border crossing because she wasn't wearing a mask. She pulled over, shot some video with her phone, and posted it on TikTok. "This isn't my country," she said. "In Canada, we're no longer free."

What Belton hadn't had to do was demonstrate proof of vaccine. This was already on the way to changing. A month earlier, Joe Biden's United States government had announced that starting in the new year, full vaccination would be required of any foreign national crossing into the U.S., including commercial truckers. Three days after Brigitte Belton posted her TikTok, Justin Trudeau's government announced it too would require truck drivers to be vaccinated as a condition of entry into Canada. The new requirement was to come into force on January 15, 2022.

At first, there seemed to be some confusion about the extent of the rule. On January 12, somebody at the CBSA told a reporter that Canadian truckers would be exempt from the vaccination requirement. The next day, three federal cabinet ministers—health, transport and public safety—issued a joint release saying the opposite.

And the day after that, January 14, 2022, a veteran protester from Medicine Hat named Tamara Lich opened a crowdfunding account on GoFundMe under the account name "Freedom Convoy 2022."

CHAPTER 3

OTTAWA

In the later days of the Rouleau Commission's testimony, Paul Champ would complain once or twice about Paul Rouleau's sense of proportion.

Champ is an experienced Ottawa labour lawyer who's represented labour unions in countless disputes up to the Supreme Court. He carries himself with confidence. His salt-and-pepper hair looks good on him. He's got a temper he kept mostly in check, but I was grateful when he flashed it because it suggested there might actually be somebody in there. He was the lawyer for something called the Ottawa Coalition of Residents and Families. On February 4, the eighth day of the convoy, a young Ottawa woman named Zexi Li had filed a lawsuit at Ontario Superior Court against the convoy's organizers and truck owners. Champ was her lawyer. Justice Hugh McLean granted her an injunction the following Monday, February 7, ordering the protesters to stop honking their damned horns. It worked, some.

On the commission's opening day, Champ told Rouleau, "I can say, commissioner, these thirty days that you have, we could have twenty-five residents line up every day to testify to tell you their stories." In fact, he would have only one day, the commission's second, to parade Ottawa residents in front of Rouleau. It was the day Rouleau began hearing witness testimony.

Weeks later, lawyers for the convoy protesters sought to add a couple more truckers to the witness list. Champ rose to grumble. This idea of even *more* time for truckers from out of town was hard to take, he said. The protesters already had a full week to tell their stories and the ordinary Ottawa residents got only a day. Really only two hours, since they had to share their day with leaders of Ottawa business groups and sympathetic city councillors. To the lawyer for the regular folks who hated the convoy, it seemed like Rouleau's priorities were out of whack.

Champ's argument had its appeal. Even at its biggest, the convoy's population was dwarfed by the population of the surrounding apartment buildings and condo towers. A string of polls suggested Canadian opinion was all on the beleaguered residents' side. A Léger poll published on February 8 said 65 per cent of respondents agreed that the convoy was a "small minority of Canadians who are thinking only about themselves and not the thousands of Canadians who are suffering through delayed surgeries and postponed treatments because of the growing pandemic." A Maru Public Opinion poll on February 17, after the Trudeau government invoked the Emergencies Act, said 66 per cent of respondents supported using that law. Abacus polled Ottawa residents specifically and found they overwhelmingly opposed the convoy, by 67 per cent to 22 per cent.

On the broader question of whether people should be vaccinated against COVID, Canadians have been even clearer: 92 per cent have had one shot, 84 per cent are considered "fully vaccinated" with two. This is far ahead of the United States (68 per cent second dose), France (79 per cent), the UK (76 per cent), Norway (76 per cent). On the question of how to fight a virus, Canadians voted with their rolled-up sleeves and it wasn't even close.

But to some extent, so what? Freedom of expression and association aren't reserved for people saying popular things. Some pollsters managed to measure a whiff of sympathy for that old-fashioned liberal sentiment. Ipsos reported that 46 per cent of respondents said that they "may not agree with everything the people who have taken part in the truck protests in Ottawa have said, but their frustration is legitimate and worthy of our sympathy."

But, again, the question facing Rouleau wasn't who was popular. It wasn't even whether the occupiers should be dispersed, but about whether they were dispersed correctly. It was whether the Trudeau government chose the appropriate legal instrument to achieve a policy goal.

In determining the answer to that question, Rouleau was under no obligation to replicate the gorgeous mosaic of Ottawa's Centretown in his hearing room. His commission was trying to understand how things went wildly wrong and whether there were better ways to right them. For that, the good people of Ottawa weren't all that germane. They weren't the reason why February 2022 in Ottawa was different from any previous February: the interlopers were. And it wasn't residents who had a mandate to anticipate, stave off, or disperse the convoy. It was the cops and politicians, and they would occupy the bulk of the commission's days.

As it happened, the two Ottawans who did get their turn under the lights did a fine job of explaining what it was like.

Victoria De La Ronde and Zexi Li sat side by side. Each swore to tell the truth. Both confirmed they were Ottawa residents living alone. De La Ronde is seventy-five and legally blind, a retired public servant. Li is twenty-one, just starting as a public servant.

What was it like when the trucks parked near their apartments and refused to leave? "The impact on my physical well-being was—is—quite extensive," De La Ronde said. She lost sleep. Her lungs hurt from the exhaust fumes. "And I also have long-term effects." Such as? "Loss of hearing. Loss of balance. Some vertigo triggered by the sound of any horn now." For weeks after the convoy ended, she heard "a phantom horn blowing."

When the trucks moved in and started honking, there was "absolutely no place for me to go" in her apartment for sleep. "I checked different rooms to see, well, maybe I can sleep on the floor. There was no place that had a diminished sound."

For Li, the effects included sleep deprivation, "and it also affected the animals that I live with, as well." Leaving her apartment was "unpleasant, to say the least." She did it anyway. "I felt almost a little bit of defiance."

She said she would be harassed for wearing her mask. Normally, she wouldn't respond. "And I think what was one of the worst things was whenever I chose not to engage . . . they would blast their horns at me with a smile on their faces. And then they would cheer in unison and almost take joy in my flinching."

People who weren't there, or who had the luxury of coming and going, can debate how serious nonstop noise and pervasive exhaust fumes might be. For De La Ronde, who walks with a white cane, there was immediate physical peril. "The sound was so high that I could not hear any chimes or signals that we use at the ends of the street to tell us that it's safe to cross," she said. "It just was not safe in my world."

Well, surely, she could order out. No. "Immediately, immediately, there was no taxi, no Uber, no Para Transpo, no grocery delivery, which I depended on."

Meanwhile, some people in Li's building started throwing eggs down onto the trucks from their windows. She was sympathetic to the egg-throwing, and unimpressed that the police came to investigate because "a complaint had been made by the truckers." What the hell was going on, she thought. "They were investigating something like this. In light of everything that was happening to us." It hardly seemed fair.

And that was the end of Li's and De La Ronde's testimony, under the gentle guidance of Natalia Rodriguez, a lawyer for the Rouleau Commission. Every witness would begin testimony with gentle guidance from commission counsel. Nobody would get a rough ride; the commission lawyers' job was largely to get witnesses to say things in person that they had already said in preliminary interviews with Rouleau's legal staff weeks before the hearings. And while most faced further rounds of questions from lawyers representing all the other parties—lawyers for the Ottawa Police Service, for civil-rights groups, and so on—most of those questions were pretty gentle, too. Brendan Miller was the lawyer for some of the convoy organizers. His clients, by and large, were Zexi Li's tormenters. At worst that gave their exchanges a sharp tone. Miller asked if Li confronted some protesters on Kent Street.

"Correct," she answered.

"And when you confronted those protesters, do you remember saying to them, which was recorded, 'Go back to where the fuck you are from?'"

"I may have said that."

The next shift at the witness stand comprised Kevin McHale, the executive director of the Sparks St. Business Improvement Association, and Nathalie Carrier, the executive director of the Vanier Business Improvement Association. Sparks Street is the hokey pedestrian mall—a storefront crêpe stand, an Inuit art gallery older than Justin Trudeau—a block south of Wellington Street, a stone's throw from Parliament. Vanier is a fourteen-minutes' drive away from Parliament Hill, but in February the convoy was right in its midst. A secondary trucker encampment, a hub for the protesters' supplies and logistics, appeared next to a sports arena out there on Coventry Road. That made the working-class Vanier neighbourhood a close-orbiting satellite of the main convoy. Most of the members of these merchant's associations would have been nearly as alarmed by long-term disruption of traffic and order as residents like Zi and De La Ronde. Maybe more so, because they had more money and their employees' livelihoods at stake.

McHale and Carrier gave the first version of a story Rouleau would hear dozens of times in the weeks that followed: the convoy wasn't taken seriously as a threat before it happened, they said, but it was overwhelming once it arrived.

A few days before the trucks started rolling in on Friday, January 27, the business groups had meetings with police and city officials. Carrier said the merchants were surprised to hear the city officials and the police were closing fewer streets than they do for a typical Canada Day and that they thought the visitors would be gone by the end of the weekend.

One of Carrier's merchant colleagues pressed the matter, asking why streets couldn't be blocked "like we do often for protester events. Why couldn't we prevent access to our core?" Police chief Peter Sloly had no real answer, says Carrier. "[He] was saying things to the order of, 'I can't stop trucks from driving in the city of Ottawa.'" Carrier found that baffling.

Soon enough, the occupiers arrived. Soon enough, they didn't leave. One of the commission lawyers asked Carrier about the mood at the Starbucks on Coventry Road in the occupation's first days. "Some protesters were perfectly pleasant and lovely," Carrier said. "That should be said. They're not all homogeneous, right? But there were definitely the ones that would make comments. . . . You know, 'The window's open, you don't need a mask,' those types of things."

At one point Carrier was on Nicholas Street, near National Defence Headquarters, shooting smartphone video of trucks parked where they shouldn't be "to demonstrate that there was lawlessness." As if to help her with her project, somebody dumped the contents of a chemical toilet in the snow.

McHale guessed that 85 per cent of businesses on Sparks Street just shut down within a day of the convoy arriving. Stores were bound by law to require customers to wear face-masks and the protesters weren't the mask-wearing type. City authorities told the stores that in the unlikely event that a bylaw enforcement officer wandered by, he'd be likelier to fine the business for permitting visitors to enter without masks than the visitors for refusing to wear masks. Another reason not to bother opening, Carrier said.

After a lunch break, the commission heard from the day's last two witnesses, Catherine McKenney and Mathieu Fleury, both members of Ottawa City Council. McKenney's Somerset Ward covers the western part of Ottawa's Centretown, Fleury's Rideau-Vanier the eastern part. Both councillors are left-leaning, smart, and experienced.

After the convoy left and before the Rouleau commission started, Fleury had announced he wouldn't run again. McKenney, who uses they and them pronouns, was running for mayor. Despite a strong campaign, their support was concentrated in the urban core of a city that covered huge stretches of ex-urban countryside. They didn't win.

The two councillors told tales much like those of Zexi Li and Victoria De La Ronde, but on a larger scale. Before the first weekend, McKenney said, Somerset Ward residents were "bracing" to get through the protest. When the first weekend refused to end, McKenney's constituents "felt that they were under a great deal of threat. Seniors reported that they had trouble going out. They felt threatened when they went into a grocery store."

One couple had a particularly nasty experience that first weekend. "There was a Pride flag in their window. Their apartment was targeted. Somebody defecated on the back step." When a pickup truck returned later in the evening, the couple left their home with a police escort.

In all this testimony, there would have been room for any observer to make a judgment call about the severity of what was being described. A commission lawyer read an email McKenney received from a resident whose apartment was permeated with noise from car horns, from 7 a.m. to 1 a.m. "My jaw hurts from clenching non-stop," the resident wrote. "I can't stop shaking. I'm barely eating and my stomach is constantly upset." How many similar emails had McKenney received from other residents? "Hundreds."

Did McKenney see any violence? "I didn't personally witness any acts of violence."

You can decide for yourself how to weigh this testimony against your personal values and sense of outrage. My own definition of violence is easily broad enough to include what the convoy inflicted on hundreds of people who couldn't escape nonstop noise and fumes in their homes for days on end. I'm aware that many of their tormentors would reply, "Well, now you know how we felt," because later in our tale we'll be hearing from those people and that is indeed what they said.

A thought experiment might help in deciding who in this tale makes you angry and how angry to be. Reverse the positions of every participant in this tale. Imagine a high-rise residential district full of Trudeau-hating blue-collar workers, besieged by hundreds of lefty city councillors for weeks on end. When they dare to venture into the street, the hapless residents are accosted on every corner by woke out-of-towners blasting air horns and shouting "Defund the police!" and "Why aren't you watching Trevor Noah?"

Does your sense of who's hurting and who's whining survive the inversion?

After Fleury and McKenney, the Rouleau commission broke for the weekend. When it reconvened on Monday, October 17, the commission's study of the convoy's impact on residents shifted to a study of the city authorities' response. Steve Kanellakos was Ottawa's city manager, essentially its top-ranking bureaucrat. Serge Arpin was the chief of staff to Mayor Jim Watson, his senior political advisor.

Kanellakos and Arpin cut contrasting figures. Kanellakos is blocky and prosaic. Everyone called him "Steve K" because, as witnesses kept explaining, nobody could pronounce his last name. I was baffled. It's Kanellakos, Can-uh-LACK-os. You had no Greek families where you grew up? For most of his half-day under oath, Kanellakos kept his hands folded on the desktop in front of him. No part of him moved except for his jaw and his eyebrows.

One of the most interesting items Kanellakos dropped on the commission was that on January 25, four days before the occupation began, he had received an email from Steve Ball, president of the Ottawa Gatineau Hotel Association. Convoy organizers had written to Ball, asking if he had hotels that would accept "a 100% occupancy rate of a minimum of 30 days to 90 days for our truckers' convoy which is approximately 10,000 members of our fleet." As if to reassure Ball, the email added that these thousands of people who were planning to stay for months were "under a strict code of conduct." Somehow city officials and the police service were still convinced they'd be clear of the protestors in a single weekend.

Arpin is slim and soft-spoken, a Cardinal Richelieu figure. His elegant façade presented an accurate but incomplete portrait, because if Jim Watson ever needed somebody to break off his whole foot in somebody's ass, Arpin was available. Every successful politician needs an enforcer. Enforcing was in Arpin's job description and, indeed, counted among his enthusiasms.

On February 11, as the convoy occupation was grinding into an unbelievable third weekend, Arpin was texting with Mike Jones, chief of staff to Marco Mendicino, Trudeau's minister of public safety, about police reinforcements. Jones was Mendicino's top political staffer, as Arpin was the mayor's.

On this particular day, Jones was encouraging Arpin to keep negotiating with representatives of the convoy leadership. This assignment grated on Arpin. He couldn't help noticing that nobody in the Trudeau government was keeping any lines of communication open with the unruly convoy. He decided to let Jones know how he felt about being handed a task the Government of Canada thought was beneath it.

"I assume that you must understand how spectacularly ridiculous the contention is that we could be meeting with them [the convoy] when your level of government trots out a number of ministers to denigrate the demonstrators and let them know that dialogue is impossible with the Government of Canada in the context of a demonstration targeting the government of Canada but somehow we should divine that we should be meeting with them to make them feel heard," Arpin typed.

"That's nauseating to say the least."

What Kanellakos and Arpin described in their testimony was a terrible loneliness at City Hall. Trudeau's government was no help. The feds wanted someone to keep talking to the protesters, but didn't want to talk themselves. So they pushed this difficult and morally precarious task down to Kanellakos, Arpin, and Mayor Watson. Ottawa's municipal police service was no help either. It had given Watson's office terrible counsel in the days before the trucks arrived and was now a tightly wound ball of infighting. Doug Ford, Ontario's premier, was especially useless. He seemed to believe Ottawa wasn't a municipality in Ontario, or that it shouldn't be.

Talking to the convoy protesters was Dean French's idea. French had been chief of staff to Doug Ford during Ford's tumultuous first two years in office. Mid-occupation, he had approached City Hall offering to make introductions to some of the convoy organizers. Watson and Arpin were reluctant, so Kanellakos first met French's connections alone. When Kanellakos was able to get a few trucks moved out of residential streets as a gesture of good faith, Arpin and Watson joined the talks.

Why were negotiations with the protesters even needed? Because everyone had been planning for a weekend-long protest and wound up instead with an unending siege.

As the days went by and the trucks didn't leave, Arpin again took out his frustration on Mendicino's chief, Mike Jones, who had been texting him reassurance. Jones said the RCMP was sending "three shifts of 70 each," or 210 Mounties to protect the good people of Ottawa. Arpin shot back: "They are lying to you flat out."

Here's how Arpin saw it: some of the promised RCMP officers had been sent to guard Rideau Hall where the governor general lives, another bunch were at the prime minister's cottage on the Rideau Hall grounds, and the rest were guarding the parliamentary precinct. Which made them all nearly useless with regard to the convoy. Traffic was flowing smoothly around Rideau Hall and the prime minister's cottage, thanks for asking. The parliamentary precinct, too, was just fine. Protesters had no designs on Parliament except to install a hot tub across the street from it.

The locations to which the Mounties were assigned reveal a striking contrast between the real problems the convoy posed to the City of Ottawa and its residents and the spectacular threats Parliament's defenders imagined. On Valentine's Day, Larry Brookson, the superintendent of operations for the Parliamentary Protection Service, noticed an increase in the number of trucks in the immediate vicinity of Parliament Hill. This was because Watson's negotiations with convoy leaders were starting to pay off. Some residential streets had been cleared, with the truckers packing in around the Hill, To Brookson, this change represented a catastrophic escalation of the threat he was paid to avoid. He emailed Kanellakos: "Quite honestly, Steve, I am at a loss as to how this sort of agreement could have been worked out with a clear disregard to security, especially considering that we just finished a bomb blast assessment which included the threat of explosive being transferred via large vehicles."

Kanellakos and Brookson were living in different worlds. The city manager was hoping to get traffic noise and exhaust fumes away from apartments occupied by people like Zexi Li and Victoria De La Ronde. Brookson was actively planning his response to what would have been the largest truck bomb in North America since Timothy McVeigh blew up the Alfred P. Murrah Federal Building in Oklahoma City.

In hindsight, it's pretty clear Kanellakos was managing a problem that had amply manifested itself, while Brookson was multiplying contingency plans for problems that hadn't, but I don't want to be too hard on Brookson. Eight years ago, a single assailant shot his way into Parliament's Centre Block and terrorized its occupants. As noted earlier, the Rideau Hall grounds had been targeted by a guy in a truck, Corey Hurren, in 2020. Protesters had absolutely stormed Germany's Reichstag and the Capitol in Washington. Brookson's job was to hope for the best but prepare for the worst. He didn't have the luxury of assuming he knew how bad the worst could get.

The Rouleau commission's tour of the City of Ottawa in crisis reached a pinnacle with the testimony of Jim Watson. Having been the city's mayor twice, from 1997 to 2000 and again since 2010, Watson was nearing the longest total tenure of any Ottawa mayor. He was testifying less than a week before the election that would choose his successor. Coming after all the others, he didn't have much to add, beyond some insights into his working relationship with Justin Trudeau and what might be called a certain tone.

First, the tone. Watson expressed the distaste many Ottawans had for the convoy crowd. For him, the convoy was an indignity visited upon his neighbours by strangers whom he would never forgive. Too much of what went on while the protesters were in town was "completely despicable behaviour," Watson said.

He repeated a story that had circulated about an incident on the convoy's first weekend at the Shepherds of Good Hope, an Ottawa

Lowertown charity that feeds and shelters people. "Having people bully their way in to get a free meal?" said Watson. "That was just abhorrent."

As it became clear the protesters didn't intend to go home soon, said the mayor, "we started to see fireworks go off, hot tubs brought in. The public, who were living here, recognized that this was a horrific situation."

Watson asked the province and the feds for police reinforcements to "kick these yahoos out of our city." He couldn't believe both levels of government gave him the runaround.

There was an almost Victorian sensibility behind Watson's comments. The convoy seemed to upset him not because of its tactical success or its drain on city resources but because he found the protestors uncouth. This theme was more prominent in his commentary than concern for his own safety. He did mention in response to a lawyer's question that he had received physical threats: "A couple people were charged. Some guy from New Brunswick was coming down here with guns in his trunk to shoot me and he was arrested." But he was there to talk about the wounds to his city's dignity. "Nothing comes close to it," he said, comparing the convoy to the rest of his political career. "You know, I think back to my first month in office, I was thrown into the ice storm. That was dramatic but it was not hurtful to people. It was difficult when people lost electricity and so on, but this was something that affected thousands of people very personally. And it was unacceptable behaviour by fellow Canadians to come into someone else's neighbourhood and act in that selfish a fashion."

Perhaps the strongest expression of Watson's distaste appeared in a "readout," a rough transcript produced by staffers at high speed, of a February 8 phone conversation between Watson and Trudeau. The prime minister begins the conversation by asking the mayor how he's doing. "A challenge for everyone," Watson says. "Still a pretty unstable situation. Nasty people out there that just don't represent Canada. Reminds me of the Republican Party down south. Can't reason with them, so vulgar, and hateful, attacking people, ripping masks off, honking their horns."

33

The conversation between the mayor and the prime minister unfolds as conversations sometimes do when the parties have contrasting agendas. Watson needed help. Trudeau just wanted to check in.

There was a three-level call coming up at 4:30 that afternoon, Watson said, a chance for federal, provincial, and municipal officials to coordinate. He reminded Trudeau what he wanted to hear from the feds at the meeting—"hopefully more resources from you on RCMP."

Trudeau fielded this clear request from a mayor in crisis by changing the subject to the government that wasn't on the call. "Have they (provincial officials) indicated they will be there at 4:30?"

Well, Watson said, it's not clear. Ontario's solicitor-general, Sylvia Jones, was being "disingenuous" with her claims to have sent 1,400 Ontario Provincial Police officers, he said.

And with that, Watson pivoted again to the message of greatest utility. He was asking for as many reinforcements from the RCMP as from the OPP and complaining that the federal bureaucracy was not acting with a sense of urgency. "Wondering what you can do to help us?"

Faced with the same question a second time, Trudeau came a little closer to answering. "One of the challenges is that it goes in steps. The first step is to go to the OPP, then RCMP. It's difficult for us to say what we need to do directly until we have a better idea of what the province is doing."

Then Trudeau changed the subject again, away from how he could deploy the vast apparatus of the federal government to help a mayor under siege. "How is your relationship with the police chief and how are you guys working together? There are moments when you are saying one thing and he is saying another, is there anything we can help around that?"

By this point, Watson had twice asked for RCMP reinforcements and twice been asked about people who weren't on the call. He swatted aside the question about Peter Sloly, the Ottawa Police Service chief, as politely as he could. "As you know PM now is not the time to change courses, we have to do our best to support [Sloly]." (The police chief would resign a week later.) Watson doggedly returned to his request for more Mounties. "I'm going to ask after this phone call whether the federal government will live up to its commitment, we need boots on the ground very shortly."

Put on the spot for the third time, Trudeau gave his clearest answer yet. "Listen, yes, you can say yes, the federal government will be there with more resources." But if Watson was hoping for details—How many boots and when?—he was again disappointed. Once more, Trudeau changed the subject: "Thing that frustrates me . . . Doug Ford has been hiding from his responsibility on it for political reasons as you highlighted, and important that we don't let him get away from that, and we intend to support you on that."

Watson by now was keenly aware that Trudeau was trying to give him the runaround. "If they keep dragging their feet, I'm happy to call them out on it," he said of Ford's government before cleverly returning to his message: "It'd be nice if we have something firmed up with the federal government to shame them."

Having failed to shake Watson, the prime minister of Canada finally consented to forward the mayor's request to the RCMP. "OK, listen obviously there are all sorts of different needs, but I will pass along all the concerns."

It wasn't a great phone call. But, again and again, we must remind ourselves that the question facing the commission wasn't whether everyone acted their best, but whether a law from an earlier epoch in Canadian history needed to be used. To Jim Watson, there was no question. "I think the prime minister did the right thing by bringing in the Emergencies Act. Because that solved our problem. It's easy to sit back and be a Monday-morning quarterback. But the people who were suffering most were the people of Ottawa. Not the people of the West Coast or the East Coast."

I'd let that be Watson's last word, but it's actually not the last thing he said. A few minutes later, he mentioned that some students he'd spoken to at Algonquin College asked him to identify the most stressful time in his recent term. "And I think a lot of them were going to say, you know, the truck convoy. And I said, 'Well actually, not to diminish the truck convoy, but it was COVID.'"

"Eight hundred people died [in Ottawa]. As a result of COVID, thousands more were seriously impacted. People lost their jobs, their livelihood. And that was a challenge that every single citizen of the world had to face. The truck convoy was a terrible experience, but it was for a set period. Three weeks. It affected dramatically the people in the inner core. But it ended. We're still dealing with COVID and we're still losing people every day."

The question Justice Rouleau was left to answer was whether the Emergencies Act was needed to resolve the second-worst crisis of Jim Watson's term, when it wasn't needed to solve the worst or any other crisis in the thirty-four years since it came into law.

CHAPTER 4

THE POLICE

How chaotic was the police response to the Freedom Convoy? Consider this: for a perilously long time during a major crisis, the besieged Ottawa Police Service barely talked to the Ontario Provincial Police and the Royal Canadian Mounted Police.

Peter Sloly, the Ottawa police chief, would sometimes say he needed so many OPP officers and so many RCMP officers for reinforcements. These announcements would come as a surprise to OPP and RCMP leadership. They had not been consulted by Sloly. They had no idea what he planned to do with those cops if delivered. So they didn't deliver them. Their forces stayed on the sidelines, mostly, and watched Sloly and the Ottawa police with mounting dismay.

On February 5, about a week into the Freedom Convoy, RCMP commander Brenda Lucki was trading smartphone texts with OPP commander Thomas Carrique. She mentioned that Justin Trudeau's federal government was losing faith in the Ottawa police. Perhaps it already had. Lucki's text wasn't entirely clear.

By February 10, the OPP and RCMP had formed an Integrated Planning Team that wasn't particularly integrated, since it was missing the Ottawa Police Service. The (not particularly) Integrated Planning Team wrote a plan for ending the occupation, a sort of here's-what-we'd-suggest-if-anyone-asked kind of thing. Its text included a devastating bullet-point assessment of the Ottawa police, which was both deliciously passive aggressive and probably worth doing in its own right. The local cops' management of the crisis was "reactive, tactical" and "aggressive," the planning team wrote; all three characteristics increased the general level of "risk." There was "no or poor partner collaboration," which was the planning team's way of saying the locals never called. Perhaps most devastating, the focus of the Ottawa police was "only maintenance and not resolution." The mess was two weeks old, as of that day, and the Ottawa police had no evident plan to stop it.

To be fair, it's not as though the Ottawa police hadn't been busy. It had descended into an orgy of infighting and contradictory actions, which took a lot of energy. The service went through four different event commanders, the designation for a senior officer with operational responsibility for handling the convoy occupation, in two weeks. Its chief of police, Sloly, would resign. That rapid turnover was a by-product of bitter internal debate over how to police a major demonstration like the Freedom Convoy. A lot of police forces elsewhere in Canada would say that debate has long since been settled. But news of the latest trends in policing hadn't reached Ottawa. So the Ottawa Police Service had to learn through trial and error in the truck-clogged streets of the capital while the world watched.

Three times in the occupation's second week, the Ottawa Police Service tried to shrink the occupation's footprint and make it less hazardous.

The first operation happened in Confederation Park, across the street from Ottawa's City Hall, on February 4. Within days after the trucks parked, some of the protesters had built a wooden shack in the park. They were also stockpiling fuel nearby. The neighbours weren't thrilled by the juxtaposition of wood and fuel, and the shack was tangible, photogenic evidence that the convoy wasn't planning on leaving soon.

The Ottawa police plan to clear Confederation Park began with the service's Police Liaison Team. Most large Canadian police forces have liaison teams. They exist to work with protesters as much as possible. All those furious Ottawa residents who were sure the police were in cahoots with the protesters? Turns out some of them kind of were.

At Confederation Park, the Police Liaison Team followed a

three-step plan, the first step of which was to urge the protesters to pack up and protest somewhere else with a little less hardware. This didn't work. The liaison team noted that some of the protesters were Indigenous. Fortunately, the team knew some Algonquin elders who were brought in to tell the protestors they should go. This didn't work either, and the liaison team had to escort the elders out of the park.

The liaison team moved to step two, which was to present the protestors with a letter from the National Capital Commission saying it was time to go or else, step three, the Ottawa police Public Order Units would clear the park. Public Order Units are the enforcers people demand when they don't like protesters. A lot of recent trends in policing have to do with using these units as a last resort. When the written notice from the National Capital Commission went up on Sunday, telling people it was time to leave, most did. The police service removed the shack without further event. It was a modest but heartening success.

The second Ottawa police operation to shrink the convoy's footprint was at the protesters' secondary tactical base on Coventry Road, a short drive from Parliament Hill, on February 6. It, too, worked, after a fashion. But because leadership had applied none of the lessons it should have learned from Confederation Park, its short-term success came at heavy cost to internal police service cohesion and to whatever trust had been built with the protesters. The third operation was planned for the intersections of Rideau Street and Sussex Drive, normally one of the busiest intersections in Ottawa's Centretown, and a place where the protesters were particularly rowdy and uncontrollable. That operation collapsed before it began, due to internal dissent within the police service that was not far from mutiny.

Sloly replaced the event commander who had made such divisive gains at Coventry and failed to win support at Sussex and Rideau on February 10. That was the very day the OPP and RCMP wrote their jilted-partner assessment of the mess in the Ottawa Police Service. And things began to improve. The new event commander, the fourth and last, was Robert Bernier. He took the job on condition that Sloly be barred from telling him what to do. He ordered the police service communication staff to stop issuing a running public tally of convoy-related arrests, because to Bernier arrests weren't the goal.

On February 11, Bernier wrote a "mission statement" that was based on the same conciliatory de-escalating logic that had produced the early success at Confederation Park. While respecting the protesters' Charter rights to assemble and protest, he would set out to "de-escalate and negotiate a peaceful resolution and demobilization" of the convoy.

The next day, February 12, Bernier's counterparts at the RCMP and OPP called him to tell him they were in town—this came as a surprise to him—and offered their assistance. In a reversal of the mulish antagonism that had characterized the Ottawa Police Service's response to the other forces until now, Bernier accepted their offer.

Within a day, drawing largely on the document the OPP and RCMP had thrown together while they were waiting for somebody to ask, Bernier and his counterparts produced an operational plan for ending the siege of Ottawa. Their plan matched the spirit of Confederation Park and the goals of Bernier's mission statement. It wasn't ready to implement, but now the three forces were working together on something worth polishing. That was Sunday, February 13. The next day, Valentine's Day, Justin Trudeau invoked the Emergencies Act.

But the story of Robert Bernier and his conciliatory spirit doesn't end there. Sloly resigned on February 15. On Thursday, February 17, Bernier and his counterparts from the OPP and the RCMP signed off on a refined, more elaborate version of their plan. And the next day, Friday, February 18, the three police forces started implementing their plan. Parliament Hill was pretty much clear within two days.

Here we approach an important question. Bernier was the Ottawa Police Service event commander for the Freedom Convoy before the Emergencies Act was invoked, and he was the event commander after. He had a plan before the act was invoked—just before, absolute-last-minute before, pulling-an-all-nighter-before-the-term-paper-submission-deadline before—and he implemented it after.

Did the Emergencies Act change anything?

What Bernier told commission lawyers who came to pre-interview him over the summer was that it hadn't. Frank Au, the commission counsel leading the questioning on the day Bernier testified, asked him to elaborate.

"The plan that I was developing was based on existing authorities, whether it be under the provincial, federal, or common-law authority to act," Bernier replied. "This is what takes place on a daily basis on those larger-type events. We have to leverage those particular authorities that exist." Before he knew the Emergencies Act would be used, "I was satisfied that we were going to have all the authorities we'd need to take action . . . in having that area cleared and the city returned to a state of normalcy."

Was the Emergencies Act *helpful*? Absolutely, Bernier said. It provides for the designation of secure zones. Which, come to think of it, he'd been planning to implement anyway. Still, all the talk about the Emergencies Act probably clarified things. "The secure zone options that were offered through the Emergencies Act was a benefit. It somewhat provided a framework, a legal framework, that would be a lot more understandable for our members, for the community and, in fact, the protesters as well."

So the act was helpful, Au offered. "Anything that contributes to mission success is a benefit," Bernier agreed.

But was it necessary? "Hard for me to say. I did not get to do the operation without it." He doesn't know what "complications" he'd have faced if he had gone into action using only common law, which can be defined as the accumulated wisdom of court decisions on countless previous police operations. But he would absolutely have gone in using only the common law. "We have used it before. We have used it since, without the Emergencies Act. And it has been effective."

The commission lawyers quizzed every police witness about two things: why they didn't know the protest would turn into a siege, and whether they thought the Emergencies Act was needed. They got varying answers to both questions. I found myself asking an altogether different question:

41

Where did these Police Liaison Teams—with their close consultation with protesters, their non-judgmental stance, their preference for negotiated outcomes instead of arrests—come from?

The other big player in major-event policing, the Public Order Units, are easy to understand. They warn and they act. They arrest. They're order over chaos. But what about this other crew?

Much of the answer came from the leader of the OPP's Provincial Liaison Team, Inspector Marcel Beaudin. He was a frustrated onlooker during the early days, when the Ottawa Police Service wasn't playing well with other police organizations. He didn't think his liaison team was being put to good use and he was startled to find the Ottawa police liaison team members sitting idle for hours instead of engaging with the protesters.

Beaudin was also the strongest advocate outside the federal government for setting up a constructive dialogue between the feds themselves and some element of the convoy leadership. Trudeau's public-safety minister, Marco Mendicino, rejected that effort and shut it down as soon as he heard about it.

I should point out that witnesses at the Rouleau inquiry had a choice before they testified. They could make a solemn affirmation that they would speak the truth. Or they could take an oath, using some religious tome—Bible, Koran, Talmud. Marcel Beaudin was the only witness to be sworn in while he held an eagle feather.

In a podcast he recorded for the OPP's members' union last autumn, Beaudin filled in a bit of his background. He has mixed ancestry, he said, and is a member of the Henvey Inlet First Nation, a tiny Ojibwe community north of Parry Sound on Georgian Bay. Beaudin also described a moment shortly after he became a police officer at age twenty-two. He went to a family wedding. While he was talking to one of the bridesmaids, "my grandmother comes over and she interrupts us as we're talking," he said. "To the young lady she says, 'I want to just let you know. You probably don't want to talk to this grandson—he's a cop. You wanna talk to my other grandson. He sells Pepsi.'"

Beaudin said he'd never had any disagreement with his grandmother

42

before. The warning wasn't personal, but I bet it stung. Her concern was over his new job. The mistrust she was expressing has to do with the often tragic and brutal history of police treatment of Indigenous Canadians. "Quite often, we were seen removing kids from families, returning children back to residential schools if they ran away," he said. "I think of the importance in our day-to-day action of restoring that trust and confidence in policing. To me, probably one of the biggest things, when it comes to policing in First Nations communities, is restoring that trust. . . . Most importantly, having the community or the people believe you have their best interests in mind."

Today, Beaudin is an inspector in the OPP's Indigenous Policing Bureau. Since 2020, he's been the Bureau's senior officer in four of its program areas. He leads investigations of missing and murdered Indigenous women and girls. He administers the Ontario First Nations Policing Agreement (OFNPA), which gives First Nations the option of designating the OPP as their local police force. And he runs an Indigenous Awareness Training unit, which teaches OPP members historical and cultural background that can help them in their interactions with Indigenous Canadians.

And, finally, Beaudin is provincial coordinator for the OPP's Provincial Liaison Team. Since 2016, he's been involved in every one of the OPP's liaison team responses to protests, demonstrations, and occupations in Ontario whether they involved Indigenous people or not.

A commission lawyer asked Beaudin: where does the Provincial Liaison Team come from? "As a result of Ipperwash," he replied.

In 1995, a few dozen members of the Stony Point First Nation occupied parts of Camp Ipperwash, a training ground for the Canadian Armed Forces and for Army Cadets. The federal government had expropriated the land from the Stony Point Chippewas during the Second World War, with promises to give it back later. Ottawa never did give the land back. So a bunch of band members camped out for weeks to remind everyone of unkept promises.

Just after Labour Day that year, the OPP staged a raid on the encampment after dark. They arrived with all the paraphernalia of no-nonsense policing, helmets, shields, Crowd Management Unit, Tactical Response Unit. Snipers. Arthur "Dudley" George, a thirty-eight-year-old unarmed Ojibwe man, was shot in the chest and killed.

The government of Premier Mike Harris had been in office for two and a half months when George was killed and refused for eight more years to hold a public inquiry into his death. The inquiry didn't begin until 2003, when the Liberals under Dalton McGuinty defeated the Conservatives and formed a new government. That was also the year Marcel Beaudin's police career began. So the repercussions from Dudley George's death have literally shaped Beaudin's career.

After this tragedy, the OPP would never again be eager to wade into a public-order dispute with riot gear and heavy weaponry. The provincial force launched an Aboriginal Relations Team (ART) to build relationships with First Nations communities before, during, and after a big demonstration. A separate Major Event Liaison Team (MELT) would do similar wraparound work for non-Indigenous protests. A couple of years later, the OPP merged the two teams into the Provincial Liaison Team. It operates on the same philosophy as liaison teams at other police services.

"When we see that there's going to be potential conflict, our job is to reach out, build relationships," Beaudin testified in front of Rouleau. "You know, sometimes people just say the word 'relationship' and they don't necessarily break that down. But to us, it actually means something."

Like what? "You need trust." Protesters need to believe that "I have their best interests in mind," he said. For them to be able to believe that, it needs to be true. They also need to believe that "ultimately, I do what I say I'm going to do, right?"

To what end? Essentially, to put the shields and helmets last, and to work together, police and protesters, to ensure they don't get used if at all possible. Liaison units seek to establish what Beaudin said is tantamount to a moral contract with the protesters: "This is the law. This is what you should avoid doing. These are some alternative options to ensure that it's lawful, peaceful, and safe." Maybe get your truck off a roadway or dismantle a fuel-burning shack because it's worrying the neighbours. "And then if there's any deviation from that, here's the potential consequences associated to that."

Those potential consequences may well include arrest. In today's OPP and in countless other police forces, trust-building liaison teams and more traditionally repressive Public Order Units work together. Good cop, bad cop, you might say. Although that's not accurate because the public order officers have a profound stake in the success of the liaison teams. And even when the Public Order Unit is needed, the liaison team keeps working to minimize the number of belligerents. "And the reason that we have those up-front conversations is because, typically, emotions and intelligence work as a teeter-totter," Beaudin testified. "If someone's emotional in times of crisis, typically, intelligence gets low."

The change in doctrine Beaudin has devoted his career to pro-moting is visible in police thinking throughout the Western world. The liaison team philosophy is embodied in the Canadian Association of Chiefs of Police's National Framework for Police Preparedness for Demonstrations and Assemblies. The framework was published in 2019 based on input by experts and practitioners across the country. Including Marcel Beaudin. "Relationship building aids in the devel-opment of respect, rapport, reciprocity, trust and empathy," the Chiefs of Police's National Framework reads.

As the Freedom Convoy approached Ottawa and throughout its occupation, there were outraged reports on Twitter and television about police who were ignoring protesters' minor infractions and actually seemed to be friendly with them. I can't speak to every case, but most of the time people were probably seeing liaison teams doing what they're designed to do: build trust and defuse tension.

This might all be hard to take for any readers who believe that what happened in Ottawa in early 2022 was an invasion by literal Nazis and that the police did everything they could to help them set up camp. I don't share that view. I think empathy had a better day on the streets of Ottawa than rote enforcement and would have done better still with an earlier start.

But in the decade and a half that liaison team philosophy has been incorporated into policing in Ontario and beyond, observers have often complained about cops who seemed to be helping protesters. For my late colleague Christie Blatchford, liaison teams, with all their rapport and empathy, amounted to a mechanism for helping Indigenous protesters tell police how to treat them. During the Idle No More protests in 2013, Ontario Superior Court Justice David Brown fumed at police refusal to immediately enforce his injunctions against rail blockades. "I do not get it," Brown wrote. "Without Canadians sharing a public expectation of obeying the law, the rule of law will shatter."

Chris Lewis, the OPP commissioner at the time, replied with a video on YouTube. Look, he said, we have this framework for critical incidents that depends on negotiation and restraint. We came up with it after Ipperwash. "These concepts and strategies, developed from experience, hard work and common sense, are difficult and complex to explain to the general public," he said. "I totally understand that."

Perhaps by now you're saying, "OK, sure, fine, restraint with Indigenous protesters is long overdue, a matter of fundamental justice, and probably honoured more often in the breach by lots of police. But mollycoddling yahoos from the sticks who didn't have the decency to get a COVID shot?"

Eric Brousseau, the Rouleau commission counsel who was questioning Beaudin, put that very question to him. "Can you just clarify for us, is this document intended to apply only to demonstrations and assemblies that touch on Indigenous issues, or is it for any sort of mass demonstration?"

"Yeah, any sort of mass demonstration," Beaudin replied.

Beaudin cited a bit of pop sociology that other witnesses cited as folklore throughout the Rouleau hearings: that in any angry crowd, 80 per cent would be law-abiding, 15 per cent would be on the fence, and 5 per cent are willing to break laws to make their point. Police liaison teams are trying to make the wavering 15 per cent stick with the law-abiding 80 per cent through appeals to reason, rather than swelling the ranks of the incorrigible 5 per cent.

He wished the Ottawa Police Service's liaison team had been in there from the first day of the siege, making little offers to the protesters, asking little favours. Seeking and offering small concessions is a means of figuring out who has influence within the larger group, whether they can be talked down from their most extreme demands and whether they will deliver a promise once made. Beaudin called these traits leadership, resolve, and compliance. And it was important to start identifying, early on, people with relatively high leadership, decent compliance, and wavering resolve. Because those traits would come in handy later.

"If someone says, 'I'm the leader of this group,' but they don't have the ability to move anyone, then you can see that right away. You wouldn't want to wait until the last minute to try and get someone to do something, recognizing that they won't have any juice in the group to actually move people."

I know this liaison team stuff is counterintuitive for people who want police to make annoying people go away, and that it's disorienting for some to learn that this philosophy comes from Ipperwash and is now being advocated in settings that could hardly be less similar. All I can say is, Marcel Beaudin has been thinking about these things endlessly for twenty years. What he learned when he got to Ottawa was that some people in the Ottawa Police Service hadn't thought about them. Mark Patterson, the event commander who wanted to help Sloly deliver some tough enforcement, had no idea how liaison teams worked. He wanted to use notes from Beaudin's Provincial Liaison Team members as evidence to get injunctions against the convoy leaders. This didn't match Beaudin's idea of building trust. "I definitely didn't want it to look like we were spying on people." Other senior Ottawa Police Service leaders had similarly limited understanding of liaison teams. One of them blamed rapid turnover in the Ottawa Police Service before and since Sloly became the chief in 2019. "We don't know how policing is done in the rest of the province because of staff turnover" is a lousy excuse.

It's not just police who need to understand liaison teams. Crowds will face police a lot more times in the next twenty years than the Emergencies Act will be used and I don't think public awareness of the options facing police in such situations is anywhere close to where it needs to be.

Days after the police finally cleared Wellington Street according to a plan Robert Bernier had drawn up without the Emergencies Act, Marcel Beaudin sent an email to senior OPP leaders asking for funding to step up training on the OPP and Canadian Chiefs of Police Frameworks for critical incidents. In Ottawa, "I would suggest without any criticism that there was a flaw in leadership due to lack of training and understanding of the tools available," he wrote. "We have not evolved as police leaders."

With thanks to Inspector Beaudin, I'll close this chapter with a question of my own. We're still talking about Ipperwash because almost thirty years ago, a rookie government and an unprepared police force viewed a deeply justifiable protest as a problem to be pushed aside. What would the next few decades in Canadian politics look like if police in Ottawa had given the Freedom Convoy a martyr?

CHAPTER 5

CONVOY TYPES

For most of two years under COVID-19 lockdown, I was my household's self-appointed chief enforcement cop. I warned my wife when I thought we were visiting the grocery store too frequently. I wouldn't let more than one of us enter the grocery at a time, because a sign in the grocery window said we shouldn't. I vetoed indoor meals with visitors from outside our bubble, when bubbles were a thing. I got a vaccine dose as soon as I could and a second dose and a third, all Moderna. Meanwhile, on social media, I watched friends abandon the great consensus, one by one.

There was the woman who runs a prominent local family business, also active in philanthropy. She sent me a link to an unlisted YouTube video of a woman mocking the notion of a Coronavirus pandemic. I wrote back critiquing the narrator's grasp of cell biology, to the extent my own memories of undergrad science permitted, pointing out that some quick Googling had established for me that the narrator was with the mob at the US Capitol on January 6, 2021 and adding that her video was hosted on the YouTube channel of a guy who swears he has witnessed Hollywood celebrities eating babies. My friend chided me for getting distracted from the real message. We stopped corresponding.

There was my friend from high school, now a yoga instructor, Earth Mother type, her politics well to the left, to the extent she has any. She wasn't going to let a foreign substance into her body. Her husband, vaccinated, left Facebook for a while because he couldn't stand what people were writing about the unvaccinated.

There was the very good pianist who lost a teaching job after he appeared in a video at the beginning of 2021, eating vegan chili with a dozen people, indoors and maskless. "Some lead between the eyes would be good" for their province's leading public-health officer, one of the guests said in the video. Today the pianist sometimes works as a Justin Trudeau impersonator at right-wing events.

There was the corporate executive who I think agrees with me on just about every element of the science of COVID but who got exhausted by the drama and jumped at a chance to move with her family to Florida.

An acquaintance who worked at a large government science organization said he routinely received emails from colleagues urging him to check the science of COVID. "These are people with PhDs," my acquaintance said. "They work here. I feel like telling them, if there's a conspiracy, we must be the ones running it."

On August 26, 2021, eleven days into a federal election campaign, the *Toronto Star* ran a front-page article about public attitudes toward people who weren't vaccinated. The display art for the article was text from tweets, blown up to headline size.

"I have no empathy left for the wilfully unvaccinated," one of the messages said. "Let them die."

"I honestly don't care if they die from COVID. Not even a little bit," said another.

The *Star's* editor later apologized, calling the story display "clumsy, poorly executed, and open to misinterpretation." The day after the *Star* story ran, in probably unrelated news, Justin Trudeau had to cancel a campaign rally after more protesters than supporters showed up to his scheduled event in Bolton, Ontario.

On January 4, 2022, three weeks before the trucks arrived on Parliament Hill, France's president Emmanuel Macron held a televised question-and-answer session with ordinary French voters. One woman complained that cancer care was being pushed back because hospitals were overcrowded with COVID patients who had refused to be vaccinated.

This was precisely the situation he was trying to fix, Macron said. "We put pressure on the unvaccinated by limiting, as much as possible, their access to social activities," he said. Over 90 per cent of people were getting vaccinated. "It's a tiny minority that resists. How can we make it smaller? Excuse me for saying it like this, but we make it smaller by pissing it off even more." The word Macron used that I've translated as "to piss off" was "emmerder"—to adorn with shit.

"I'm not here to piss off the French," he continued. "I bug the administration all day long when it gets in people's way. Well, here, the unvaccinated, *j'ai très envie de les emmerder*." Or, I'm very much in favour of pissing them off.

Vaccine opponents were guilty of "an enormous moral error," Macron continued, because they "sap the solidity of a nation. . . . When my liberty threatens the liberty of others, I become irresponsible. An irresponsible person is no longer a citizen."

I drag Macron into all of this again because he expressed more eloquently the sentiment that animated our local authorities. It's worth mentioning that he was, in fact, a late convert to the cause of pissing people off. COVID restrictions in France were, through 2021, often more relaxed than in Canada.

Macron's example seemed briefly to inspire his Canadian counterparts. Six days after the French president used a bad word on television, Quebec premier François Legault announced the province would require a "health contribution," essentially a substantial targeted tax, from Quebecers who refused to be vaccinated.

This idea was fraught with logistical challenges. Big ones. For starters, Legault's health department would have been forbidden by law from sharing data on vaccination status with his revenue department. He eventually dropped the idea. But the instinct was one Macron would have recognized: since a disproportionate share of the load on Quebec's health care system was being caused by unvaccinated people who had recklessly contracted COVID, the state should make them pay.

Macron's vocabulary and Legault's policy temptations were of a piece with the Trudeau government's last-minute reversal on whether Canadian citizens would be exempted from the vaccination requirement for cross-border trucking. All three leaders participated in a punitive zeitgeist that was entirely understandable for public officials whose goal was to reduce the number of unvaccinated citizens from few to none. All three happened in January 2022, while a bunch of Canadians who came pre-loaded with resentments against the Trudeau government were wondering whether or not to do something about it.

It turns out that when you set out to piss people off, they get pissed off. Sorry for the salty language. It's French.

You might say, all any of these people ever had to do was get vaccinated. And it's true. But there has never been a vaccination drive that was universally welcomed and the reasons for opposing vaccination are rarely only public-health reasons.

In 1885, smallpox killed 3,234 people in Montreal, nearly 2 per cent of the city's population. Historian Michael Bliss wrote a book about it: *Plague, a History of Smallpox in Montreal* (1991). My former colleague John Geddes wrote about Bliss's book in *Maclean's* magazine in 2021, when vaccine hesitancy was suddenly back in the news. The 1885 outbreak happened when vaccines against the smallpox virus had been available for nearly ninety years. Most English-speaking Montrealers, concentrated in the western part of the city, got vaccinated. Far fewer francophones in the east end followed suit. Francophones, mostly young children, suffered 90 per cent of Montreal's smallpox deaths.

The 1885 pandemic was deeply political, the parish against the business elite, with all that entailed. The French press did not take the smallpox outbreak seriously and was scornful of "sensation-seeking" English newspapers. Vaccine skepticism was near synonymous with the struggle against the English elite: "You resisted the oppressors and all their works."

This was not an isolated case of science conflicting with politics. Conflict between science and politics is the way of the world. In her 2015 book *Vaccine Nation: America's Changing Relationship with Immunization*, Berkeley health-care historian Elena Conis tracks the history of vaccine hesitancy. Conis is no vaccine skeptic. But she knows that appeals to science have never been universally persuasive, because social and political trends affect the willingness of different people to believe what different governments tell them.

Anti-vaccination groups in the nineteenth century, she writes, viewed compulsory vaccination as "un-American for its violation of fundamental freedoms." But the rise of the United States as an economic, industrial, and scientific power through most of the twentieth century coincided with increasingly ambitious vaccination drives that were largely welcomed in the spirit of the era. Think of the polio vaccination drives of the 1950s, with its "Salk Hops"—the price of entry to a teenage dance was agreeing to get a jab. But as political life grew more complex and fraught in the 1960s and 1970s, "feminism, environmentalism, and other social movements . . . challenged scientific and governmental authority," Conis writes.

This was the surprise for me in Conis's account, given that the opponents to COVID restrictions mostly occupied the spectrum from "fairly conservative" to "quite far right." In the age of Vietnam, Silent Spring, and Watergate, much of the opposition to government immunization programs came from what was then a burgeoning political left.

An early breach in the postwar consensus for widespread immunization appeared among America's mothers, who in a more patriarchal era were presumed to be the ones responsible for making sure Junior had his shots. Magazines aimed at women readers were generally careful to reinforce federal messaging. "Misguidedly, some of us fear that vaccines are dangerous," *Harper's Bazaar* wrote in 1976, "but the minimal risk must be weighed against the much greater benefit." But *Mothering*, a magazine about "natural family living" founded in Colorado in 1976, often printed letters from readers who doubted that even Jimmy Carter's administration knew what was best for their children. "The magazine's writers warned those allergic to eggs and chickens to avoid the measles vaccine," Conis writes. "They informed readers that vaccinating a child against polio could cause the disease in other family members. And they listed encephalitis and death as possible side effects of the pertussis vaccine. These warnings, noted the editors, were taken directly from vaccine package inserts." Readers were invited to "do their own research" rather than accept the dictates of authority.

In the late 1970s and early 1980s, as the Carter presidency led to Ronald Reagan's, Cold War politics came into play in the debate over vaccines, along with the usual conservative rhetoric of personal freedom. Barbara Syska, who'd been born in Poland, sued her Maryland school board after her son was expelled for not being vaccinated. "I'm a refugee from a communist country," she said. "There the good of the largest number of people is important, not the individual. I came here where the individual is supposed to have a say."

Later in the 1980s, environmentalist rhetoric accompanied vaccine hesitancy. A soft-spoken naturopathy advocate and best-selling author, Robert Mendelsohn, wrote in *How to Raise a Healthy Child . . . in Spite of Your Doctor* (1984) that vaccines might be a "medical time bomb" because "no one knows the long-term consequences of injecting foreign proteins into the body of your child."

And so on. When AIDS was spreading fast and an almost-certain death sentence, some people warned that vaccines weakened the body's natural immune function. When diagnoses of psychiatric disorders among children and teenagers became commonplace, some blamed school immunization programs.

Depending on the era, then, vaccines met opposition because they were a tool of Anglo oppression in Montreal, because they clipped freedom's wings, because they contradicted maternal instincts, because they were Communist, because they weren't natural, because they would wreck your immune system, or because they would make your teenager depressed.

It seems that people who were angry about vaccines were almost always angry about other stuff, too. As were the Ottawa occupiers. It's been noted that the Freedom Convoy had precursor events that predated the coronavirus, like United We Roll in 2019. It's fair to wonder, then, whether the convoy was really about vaccination requirements for truckers, given that most of the convoy protesters weren't truckers and most truckers were happily vaccinated. One might ask whether the convoy was about vaccines at all. Maybe it was just about hating Justin Trudeau. Clearly, for most of the protesters, to some extent it was both.

You might be thinking: "Sure, there's been unease about vaccination over the years. But none of those moms or environmentalists or crackpot naturopaths hopped into trucks and rode to Ottawa to overthrow the government." Which is true. But if their testimony can be taken at face value, neither did many of the Freedom Convoy organizers.

Keith Wilson, for example, flew.

Wilson is a bespectacled, well-spoken lawyer from Edmonton. He's been practicing for twenty-eight years, often for "people who are up against forces bigger than them." That has sometimes meant ranchers fighting oil companies. It has often meant just about anybody fighting government. Wilson's wife, a retired nurse, generally wishes he would work less. But in fall 2021 she got so upset about anti-COVID restrictions that she urged him to sue some government for something. He picked travel restrictions.

Wilson's interrogator in the Winifred Bambrick Room was Jeff Leon, the commission's co-lead counsel. How's that travel case going, he asked. "We just got struck on mootness," Wilson said mournfully. (Translation: the case was thrown out because the restrictions Wilson wanted to contest were no longer in effect.) "We're appealing that to the federal Court of Appeal."

Wilson told the commission that on February 1, 2022, he was on a Zoom call about the travel case with his clients at the Justice Centre for Constitutional Freedoms, a Calgary group that makes Charter arguments in court cases on behalf of social conservatives. Wilson noticed there were more people on the call than usual. Some of the convoy protesters were looking for lawyers. By the next morning, he was on a flight to Ottawa.

That was quick, Leon said. "Well, I got spousal consent very quickly, so that helped tremendously," Wilson said.

The flight was a chartered twin-prop. It took its time getting to Ottawa, with stops in Medicine Hat, Regina, Saskatoon, Winnipeg, and Thunder Bay to pick up other lawyers and an accountant. Why a charter? "Some of the passengers were unvaccinated." How about Wilson? "I'm double vaccinated."

So on February 2, late at night, he arrived at ARC The Hotel, an elegant boutique hostelry with an affected name on Slater Street, three blocks from Parliament Hill. It had become a logistical base for a bunch of convoy organizers. The rest of Wilson's night was spent meeting people—it was essentially his first encounter with the leadership— and getting several of them to sign retainers so he could be their lawyer.

He never did meet James Bauder, the Alberta trucker whose so-called memorandum of understanding called for the governor general and the Senate to eliminate COVID-related restrictions in cooperation with Bauder's group, Canada Unity. But, being a lawyer, he was asked about it by other convoy protesters all the time.

The memorandum of understanding was essentially a badly written formula for a coup. It gathered hundreds of thousands of signatures online, but it had few fans among the convoy organizers. To Wilson, the memorandum was "legal nonsense." He explained this "consistently and repeatedly."

In the next chapter, we'll look at the Trudeau government's response to the convoy and see that, to the government, the occupiers were a tightly knit and strongly determined bundle of malevolence that could not possibly be spoken to. What you learned on hearing these people speak, however, was that they were a bunch of strangers who disagreed about many things. As a bonus, the ones who had read some law understood that this plan with the governor general and the Senate was risible.

Also, many of them were eager for somebody in a position of authority to speak with them.

In that long first week of February, Peter Sloly, the Ottawa police chief, was under increasing pressure from politicians and the public to make headway against the occupiers. Wilson was hearing from his new clients, the organizers, that the mood on the street was tense. He called another client looking for ideas. That client was Brian Peckford, who was the highly eccentric premier of Newfoundland a million years ago. These days he lives on Vancouver Island and fits right in. He was the lead plaintiff in that challenge to travel restrictions that was eventually struck for mootness.

Wilson asked whether Peckford knew anybody who could find him somebody to talk to. He did! Soon Wilson received a call from Dean French.

French had been chief of staff during Doug Ford's first two years as premier of Ontario. It was a rocky period, but any premier's chief of staff will know people in the city halls of the province's larger cities. French knew people in Jim Watson's Ottawa City Hall.

As he drew this narrative out of Wilson on the witness stand, Jeff Leon asked him why talking was such a priority. "I've been in emergency operations centres of government on two major incidents and I've seen the chaos that occurs in there," Wilson said. "And, you know, I know the importance of dialogue and communication. And I can sense the danger of the parties not talking, even if it's [only] back-channel."

French and Wilson had "a very, very intense phone call where he was testing me and I was testing him," Wilson recalled. "Once he learned to trust me and I learned to trust him, we both thought it was achievable, so then he proceeded to go to work."

Four days later, Wilson was at a meeting at Ottawa City Hall with Steve Kanellakos, the city manager. Wilson testified that he opened the conversation by trying to find something to offer. "If we can move trucks and protesters, where can we provide the most immediate and effective relief?"

Steve K and the other City of Ottawa people at the meeting were particularly concerned about the intersection of Sussex Drive and Rideau Street. Fine, said Wilson and the other convoy reps. They left, promising to keep the meeting secret. "In these situations, it's always about building trust and it's the littlest things you can control that build the trust," Wilson testified. "And so we agreed to keep the meeting secret."

Then Wilson and Eva Chipiuk, another lawyer for the convoy, and Tom Marazzo, a retired Canadian Armed Forces captain who was handling logistics for the convoy, went in a straight line from the meeting to the intersection of Rideau and Sussex. "If something needed to be done, you did it right there and then," he testified. "You never waited."

Wilson and Chipiuk and Marazzo arrived at the intersection and looked around. It was obvious right away why you'd want that intersection cleared. On one corner there's Ottawa's biggest downtown shopping mall. On another is a top-tier condo building. The US Embassy and the Senate (temporarily relocated) are each half a block away.

The three convoy organizers worked out a little charade where Wilson, who'd been on television and might hope to have some profile, left the scene and went to the Sheraton hotel while Chipiuk and Marazzo tried to get the truckers at Rideau and Sussex to move. "We had so little to negotiate with in terms of tools and tactics with the protesters," Wilson testified. So the other two could try to get the Rideau-Sussex truckers to move, and if that didn't work, they could say, "Well, I guess we're going to have to get Keith." Then he'd show up, a relative celebrity, and everyone would be suitably impressed.

Milling with the crowd, Chipiuk and Marazzo found that the first three trucks blocking traffic at Rideau and Sussex were driven by Polish Canadians. Luckily, Chipiuk speaks Polish. Soon there was a plan to unblock at least the westbound lanes. But there were concrete traffic barriers in the way. The police needed to get those barriers moved. All of this took longer than it's taking me to tell you, but it was going in the right direction, toward de-escalation, with many good lessons in leadership, resolve, and compliance all around.

Then one of the Ottawa police liaison officers received a phone call. "The deal's off," he said. "They're not going to move the barricades." This was during the period where Mark Patterson was the police service's event commander and he was trying to establish himself as a strong enforcer on behalf of the beleaguered Chief Sloly. And that was that.

Wilson spent the rest of the occupation trying to regain lost momentum. Maybe he and his conciliatory colleagues could invite most of the truckers to relocate to some small town well outside Ottawa, providing them an excellent excuse to go home, and maybe that would lead somebody in the federal government to meet with some of the organizers. The somebody could have been a senior bureaucrat. It didn't have to be Trudeau. "There was not a strong desire to have a meeting with the prime minister."

As plans go, it was sketchy, and perhaps the most important thing to note was that before Wilson could get anywhere close to implementing it, the Emergencies Act and several waves of suddenly better-coordinated police relieved him of the necessity of trying. What's most striking to me is how far the protesters were from resembling any kind of cohesive force. Which leaves me wondering what might have happened if the factions that were urging cooperation on every side—Kanellakos at city hall, Marcel Beaudin at the OPP, Wilson and Marazzo and Chipiuk among the protesters—had managed to line up a few good days in a row.

Maybe there was no way that could have happened. Robert MacKinnon, a federal government lawyer, asked Wilson about the chaos within the convoy. "You have also said that the convoy attracted a lot of strange people." Wilson agreed that it had.

MacKinnon: "And in those people you mention the coven of witches?"

Wilson: "That's what they called themselves and they were doing weird séance things and burning things in the lobby."

MacKinnon: "And conspiracy groups like Diagolon and QAnon?"
Wilson: "You bet."

All these weirdos came to Ottawa "like moths to a flame."

Tom Marazzo, the military veteran who ran logistics for the convoy, testified after Wilson. There was no ordering any of them around, he said. "I had no legitimate or legal authority to tell anyone to do anything and I wasn't signing anyone's pay cheque. This was a case where you—you know, you had to use your soft skills to communicate and get people to buy in with what you were trying to do collectively."

Maybe even with all the faith and luck in the world, getting this bunch of people do anything, even from within, would have been like picking up a handful of water.

Before turning to the federal government, the organization that worked hardest to maintain its splendid isolation from the emmerdés, three more observations on the general theme of listening vs. pissing off.

First, on February 1, the day Keith Wilson boarded a twin-prop flight for Ottawa, Quebec premier François Legault abandoned his plan for a tax on unvaccinated Quebecers. He claimed he wanted "to make progress for Quebec in a serene social climate." He said, "I'm calling on everyone to put a bit of water in their wine. Let's try to talk to one another and bring Quebecers together so we can eventually turn the page."

At the time, it seemed to me that Legault was giving in to blackmail. A separate convoy of truckers was heading to Quebec City. Cancelling public-health measures to appease these folks seemed counterproductive. Later, I remembered that Legault's tax on the unvaxxed would have been impossible to implement and that it seemed designed to flatter the vaccinated as much as to persuade those who weren't. Whatever Legault was trying to accomplish, pissing people off seemed less useful at the beginning of 2022 than it might have at the end of 2021.

Second, this whole thing was, in part, about whether listening to a bunch of malcontents would do anyone any good. The way things worked out, one man was vocationally required to listen to every word the convoy witnesses had to say. His name was Paul Rouleau. His report speaks about the protesters with a striking measure of empathy. "COVID-19 health measures had a profound impact on many Canadians. Businesses were closed and livelihoods were lost. Families and friends could not meet in person. Children could not go to school. People died in hospitals and long-term care homes at times when their loved ones were not allowed to visit them. The protesters who testified at the hearings spoke passionately about the impacts of COVID-19 and how, from their perspective, the desire for change to these rules was a driving force behind the protests. I accept that this was the case."

Of course, Rouleau's report is not an ode to the heroism of the common man. "There was disregard for both the law and the well-being of the people of Ottawa," he writes. [T]he organizers did not do all they could do to limit the amount of violence and harassment." On the evidence, Paul Rouleau is very much an on-the-one-hand, on-the-other kind of guy. But he doesn't dismiss the convoy leaders outright because he couldn't, for the simple reason that he saw and heard them.

Third, a week after Legault scrapped his unworkable tax on the unvaccinated, the ranks of les emmerdés swelled briefly by one more person. One more person became so pissed off he decided to take unusual measures. That person was the Liberal MP for the Quebec City riding of Louis-Hébert, Joël Lightbound.

Lightbound didn't climb into the cabin of an eighteen-wheeler. He climbed behind the microphone of a news-conference room on Parliament Hill and for an hour made more noise than any trucker's horn. "Nazi flags and Confederate flags have no place in Canada," he began. "I also wish to denounce the far-right groups that we have seen in these protests." Then the pivot.

Lightbound said that on television he'd seen "an interview with what seemed to be a very kind grandmother who demonstrated for her grandkids. She looked and sounded nothing like a white supremacist. Nor did the black, Sikh, and Indigenous Canadians I saw demonstrating on my way to Parliament these last two weeks or in Quebec City this last Saturday. I have enough respect for my fellow Canadians not to engage in these easy and absurd labels."

He continued. "I've heard from parents worried to see their kids sink into depression and slowly lose their joy of living. I've heard from pediatricians in tears telling me about their young patients' despair, anxiety, isolation, as well as the stunning increase in school dropouts they are observing."

Why, with one of the most highly-vaccinated populations in the world, were Canadians so divided, he asked. "The World Health Organization recently recommended dropping or alleviating many border measures, including vaccine requirements, as they've proven to be ineffective in fighting the propagation of the Omicron variant. That's the World Health Organization."

Lightbound's statement was turning into a nearly unprecedented attack on the Trudeau government's way of governing, delivered from within the Liberal caucus itself. Too many Canadians believe the government is unwilling "to adapt so as to reflect the changing data and the changing reality of the pandemic of the world," Lightbound said. "They're worried that measures which ought to be exceptional and limited in time are being normalized with no end in sight, like vaccine passports, mandates and requirements for travellers."

At last, Lightbound's critique shifted from Trudeau's manner of handling the pandemic to his way of winning elections—perhaps the most personal criticism that could be levelled against this most election-obsessed of leaders. "I think it's time to stop dividing Canadians, to stop pitting one part of the population against another," Lightbound said. "I can't help but notice with regret that both tone and the policies of my government changed drastically on the eve and during the last election campaign.

"From a positive and unifying approach, a decision was made to wedge, to divide and to stigmatize. I fear that this politicization (of) the pandemic risks undermining the public's trust in public-health institutions."

Having made headlines by spewing himself like nine yards of toothpaste, Lightbound worked hard in the days that followed to reinsert himself back into the tube. He has not since revisited the remarks he made in that extraordinary news conference. He remains today a Liberal MP as unremarkable as the others, although sophisticated instruments would probably measure a glow surrounding the Quebec City MP that his colleagues lack. Once, without warning, on what turned out to be his thirty-fourth birthday, he spoke for himself. The possibility that he might do so again can never be ruled out. And, when he spoke, he said things the pissed-off mobs in the streets might have recognized.

In his 1970 essay *Voice, Exit and Loyalty*, the economist Albert O. Hirschman wrote that members of any organization have two broad options when the organization's output starts to decline in quality: they can speak up or they can leave. Hirschman called these options "voice" and "exit." The members—employees, clients, citizens, depending on the nature of the organization—make complex calculations about when to use voice and when to exit. When either option's benefits are limited, the other option becomes more attractive.

The Freedom Convoy can be understood as an act of exit by people who felt they had been denied a voice. A few of them thought they still deserved a voice and sought a venue for exercising that option. But Joël Lightbound sits facing the Prime Minister of Canada every Wednesday in the Liberals' national caucus meeting. If he felt his own voice had been so degraded that he had to act out a one-day pantomime of exit, what hope to be heard do the rest of us have?

CHAPTER 6

DECISION TIME

A friend of mine who worked closely with the Trudeau government before gently falling out with it said that it typically gets the big things right and screws everything else up. It is easily distracted, but its power of concentration, when it knows it needs to concentrate, is considerable. He listed two "big things." The first was the Trump presidency. The US didn't invade and NAFTA was substantially salvaged after two years of negotiations, in which the Prime Minister's Office was very much hands-on. The second was COVID. Canada suffered fewer deaths than most comparable countries, largely because Justin Trudeau was able to use budgetary room made available by the discipline of his four predecessors to pay Canadians to stay home.

If only the India trip, the Aga Khan vacation, the Tofino vacation, the Canada Infrastructure Bank, the seven years of paralysis on renovations to 24 Sussex, the WE Charity, the inability to pick a lane on relations with China, and the loss of two ministers over SNC Lavalin hadn't gotten in the way, this government would be a great success.

What became clear over the ten days of testimony by federal government witnesses at the Rouleau Commission was that the Freedom Convoy wasn't treated with the care reserved for legacy-defining "big things" by this government, but the Rouleau Commission was. In February 2022, when the truckers were holding court on Wellington Street, there was federal stumbling and hesitation aplenty.

In November, when Paul Rouleau was holding court on Wellington Street, Team Trudeau recovered its gift for extended choreography.

Cabinet ministers arrived fully briefed and ready to punch out their message lines. "I was being prudent," David Lametti, the justice minister, said in response to a question. He would repeat the word "prudent" four more times in a 200-word answer. Deputy ministers referred to elements of testimony that would come up a week in the future. Everybody who would testify kept tabs on what everyone else was saying. At the Halifax International Security Forum, Jody Thomas, Trudeau's national security advisor, listened to the proceedings with an earphone in one ear so she could listen simultaneously to the testimony of Janice Charette, the clerk of the privy council, in front of Rouleau.

Even Justin Trudeau, when he became the last witness on November 25, went in with both broad and specific assignments. He needed to be credible as a thoughtful statesman acting in the nation's best interest. Opinions vary, but his testimony received better reviews than almost any other public appearance he's made. He was also batting cleanup after everyone else in his government had spoken, so he needed to tie up two loose ends. First, reinforce that the events of early February met the Emergencies Act's test for a public-order emergency. Second, erode the claim that the Ottawa police had finally gotten their act together by February 14 and didn't need emergency powers to finish off the convoy.

That the extraordinary fleet of federal government witnesses was so seamlessly coordinated was testimony to the importance of their task. Usually, the first draft of history is written in a hundred places at once, but here it would be written by Paul Rouleau, and they needed to impress him. That there were so many federal government witnesses (thirty-three, nearly half of all the witnesses Rouleau would hear) suggests that Trudeau's advisors liked their chances.

These were the all-stars. Trudeau, sure, but also Chrystia Freeland, who carries the nuclear football of the prime minister's credibility with her at all times. Katie Telford, who will soon pass Jean Chrétien's college classmate Jean Pelletier as the longest-serving prime ministerial chief of staff in history. David Lametti, who had hardly spoken in public since a battlefield promotion saw him replace Jody Wilson-Raybould as Canada's attorney general. The aforementioned Janice Charette. And Michael Sabia, Freeland's deputy minister of finance, whom Trudeau had handpicked for a key public service appointment when he thought the post-COVID future would look like boundless opportunity instead of inflation, war in Europe, and a dog-eat-dog battle for foreign investment.

Every government becomes more secretive with time and Trudeau has had lots of time. He would not flash this much talent lightly, much less subject his people to questions from lawyers who know how to ask them, unlike, say, opposition MPs. Still less would he relish having their private correspondence and their cabinet documents projected on screens while they spoke.

In fact, if future governments pause before invoking the Emergencies Act a second time, it probably won't be because they fear the "very high threshold for invocation" that Paul Rouleau mentioned in his report before declaring that Trudeau surpassed that threshold. It will more likely be because they won't want their laundry aired by some future judge in some future commission of inquiry.

What kind of laundry?

Rouleau saw rough transcripts of two Trudeau phone conversations, one with Ottawa mayor Jim Watson and one with Ontario premier Doug Ford. Trudeau's office sends out vapid happy-face "readouts" of his phone calls with other world leaders all the time, but had never mentioned these two calls.

Rouleau was told that a phone conversation with US President Joe Biden came together so quickly that the Canadians were deeply worried, because it normally takes weeks or months to get on the big guy's call list. That's an admission of Canada's place in the pecking order that no government has made before.

Rouleau saw extensive transcripts of cheerful text exchanges among ministerial political staffers, many of whom had not graduated from university when Trudeau became prime minister, over "narrative" and "framing," considerations governments prefer to pretend are beneath them.

And was there a glint of merriment in Paul Rouleau's eye as Shantona Chaudhury read aloud a text message from Alberta premier Jason Kenney to Trudeau's intergovernmental minister Dominic LeBlanc? "Your guy has really screwed the pooch," Kenney wrote. "This trucker vax policy is obviously just dumb political theatre. Calling them all Nazis hasn't exactly helped. And now the provinces are holding the bag on enforcement. I can't get any heavy equipment from private vendors to move these freakin' trucks off the border because the crazies are making death threats, and you guys turned down our request for army equipment to help us. Because apparently the Government of Canada doesn't really care about the international border being closed. Pensive emoji." Hearing a lawyer say "pensive emoji" out loud was a highlight of the festivities.

Kenney continued: "But don't worry, the RCMP commander in Alberta just told me proudly that he has secured some psychologists to do a profile assessment on the protesters. I said, 'That's great news, deputy commissioner. Do you any of them know how to drive a tow truck.' J."

LeBlanc, we learn, had forwarded this exchange to Omar Alghabra, the minister of transport, who wrote back: "Speaking of bonkers." LeBlanc replied, "Totally." It's sad that no one in Ottawa appreciates great prose.

One of the first federal witnesses was Brenda Lucki, the commissioner of the RCMP. She would end up announcing her retirement shortly before Rouleau released his report, although he said nothing particularly scorching about her. On the stand, she peered out from over the top of a face mask, an increasingly rare accessory, and spoke in a low, even voice. She denied having strong recollections of specific moments during February's unpleasantness. It may simply have been information overload. She was often giving three briefings a day to deputy ministers, cabinet committees, and the prime minister himself.

"Oh my goodness!" she said at one point, when commission lawyer Gordon Cameron urged her to try harder. "I don't think people understand the amount of meetings we had. There were so many meetings."

Fortunately, electronic records of some meetings survived. They suggest Lucki was a gifted multitasker, often participating in a simultaneous Teams chat with police colleagues while she waited to speak to her elected and bureaucratic counterparts. In some cases, the meetings themselves were forgotten but the chats endured.

"I need to calm him done," she wrote to colleagues during one supper-hour cabinet committee meeting on February. 5. She meant "calm him down." This does not appear to have gone well. "ok so calm is not in the cards" she wrote fourteen minutes later. Who was refusing to calm down? Mark Flynn, the RCMP's assistant commissioner for national security and protective policing, typed a strong hint a minute later: "When the AG talks like this, we better get our own plan going . . ." Taken together, the two senior police officers' notes suggested the attorney general, David Lametti, was in a rare mood as the convoy entered its second weekend.

This information dovetailed with a document tabled several weeks earlier, a transcript of a text-message exchange between Lucki and Thomas Carrique, the commissioner of the Ontario Provincial Police. That conversation, too, happened on February 5. It was the conversation where she revealed to Carrique that the feds were losing, or had already lost, their faith in Peter Sloly. The time stamps and the content suggest that Lucki was Teams-chatting with her RCMP colleagues while she phone-texted with Carrique, in the middle of virtual meeting with cabinet ministers. "Trying to calm them down, but not easy when they see cranes, structures, horses, bouncing castles in downtown Ottawa," she told Carrique, minutes after commiserating with Flynn about Lametti.

By February 13, calm was still not in the cards. Trudeau had convened an Incident Response Group (IRG). Unlike most cabinet committees, IRGs are decision-making bodies with the prime minister attending. This one had a vital decision to make: whether to invoke the Emergencies Act for the first time in its existence.

While she waited to give her assessment to the IRG, Lucki kibitzed with RCMP colleagues via Zoom. The transcript of the Zoom chat begins in mid-afternoon and ends well after 10 p.m. While she waited, Lucki speculated with Flynn about the effect invoking the act might have.

Flynn: "I would be curious what our psychologist, that informed our plan, thinks about the reaction . . ."

Lucki: "reaction by who."

Flynn: "reaction of the protesters. Government giving themselves more power . . . The protest started due to government exerting power."

Lucki: "great observation." And less than a minute later, "it could deepen division."

An hour later, Lucki had given up hope of making her report. "So doesn't look like I will be reporting on anything."

The meeting ended without hearing from Lucki and Justin Trudeau would invoke the act the next day.

Marco Mendicino's chief of staff had asked Lucki on February 12 for a list of Emergency Act powers that would come in handy. She produced the list and, in a burst of initiative, also answered a question that Mendicino's office hadn't asked: "This said, I am of the view that we have not yet exhausted all available tools that are already available through the existing legislation. . . . These existing tools are considered in our existing plans and will be used in due course as necessary."

Lucki seems not to have been particularly bothered that the prime minister and several colleagues were hurtling toward a decision she disagreed with without benefit of her counsel. But Jody Thomas was.

Thomas was deputy minister of National Defence for several years before becoming Trudeau's national-security advisor. She was the highest-ranking official with operational responsibility for responding to the convoy. In her own testimony, two days after Lucki's, she made it clear she wasn't impressed with an RCMP commissioner who didn't show up for the big game. "Individuals who are at that meeting are expected to provide information that is of use to decision makers . . . the prime minister and his cabinet," Thomas said. "If there is useful or critical information it needs to be provided, whether you are on the speaking list or not."

Lucki hadn't put her views on record. Nor had she given Thomas or the IRG details about the first plan the Ottawa police had concocted with the OPP and the RCMP—the plan Robert Bernier had cooked up at light speed with input from the other forces when he became Peter Sloly's fourth event commander for the convoy.

"There was no evidence there was a plan," Thomas testified. "We had been told there was a plan multiple times."

Thomas's testimony was largely an account of how lousy information-sharing on national security was, even without Brenda Lucki's help. Thomas had never heard of the OPP's well-regarded Project Hendon reports, which had intelligence on the convoy's progress before the trucks arrived in Ottawa. In fact, she still hadn't heard of the Hendon reports when the trucks left.

Thomas said the federal national-security apparatus couldn't analyze so-called open-source intelligence (i.e., follow what was happening on social media) because of siloed organizational structures and a lack of in-house expertise.

She also said the public service had no dedicated, longstanding, integrated office for assessing domestic national-security threats. In the last few days before Trudeau invoked the Emergencies Act, she had told the Intelligence Assessment Secretariat, whose job was to keep an eye on global threats, that she needed it to pitch in on what was happening down the street. This probably wasn't ideal. Russia, as it turned out, was days away from a full-scale invasion of Ukraine. It's not as though all was quiet on the global-threat front.

One measure of the chaos in Ottawa's intelligence-gathering activity was the frantic email Thomas sent to several federal officials on the morning of February 14, hours before Trudeau invoked the Emergencies Act. "I need an assessment for Janice about the threat of these blockades," Thomas wrote (Janice was Janice Charette, clerk of the Privy Council). "The characters involved. The weapons. The motivation. Clearly this isn't just COVID and is a threat to democracy and rule of law. Could I get an assessment please."

Thomas's intention was to pass the assessment to the prime minister of Canada on one of the most important days of his career. People on the email's distribution list asked Thomas how specific she wanted them to be, so twenty minutes later she sent a second email. "This about a national threat to national interest and institutions. By people who do not care about or understand democracy. Who are preparing to be violent. Who are motivated by anti government sentiment."

Funny thing about what Thomas testified was to be a "last formal document . . . laying out the entire spectrum of threat." It never arrived. There was no final threat assessment. "I think it fell through the cracks and we were overtaken by events."

Was the comment in the second email about the protesters "preparing to be violent" invented from nothing? No. Was it rock solid? Also no.

I haven't said much about the other blockade at Coutts, but on February 14, the day after the IRG meeting, events took an alarming turn. The RCMP seized thirteen long guns and a lot of ammunition and made three arrests. There would be more arrests later. Charges included conspiracy to commit murder.

Perhaps the most important thing about the weapons cache was that as soon as it was discovered, the Coutts blockade collapsed. The main group of protesters were horrified at the presence of serious firepower in their midst. They lined up to hug the Mounties who had been watching them warily and then went home.

But that happy conclusion didn't come until the day Trudeau invoked the act. Mendicino, in his testimony, was more focused on the part about the deadly weapons than the part about the bulk of the protesters going home. "For me, this represented, far and away, the most serious and urgent moment in the blockade to this point in time," he testified.

Whatever Lucki might have said if she had put her virtual hand up while Zooming into the February 13 IRG meeting, what she actually wrote to Mendicino and Thomas moments before the meeting started was an email about disturbing news from Peterborough.

"You may have heard that a tractor trailer with approximately 3,400 firearms was stolen overnight in Peterborough," she wrote. "The firearms are reported to be .22 calibre rifles. . . . We don't know if it is related to the current protest but I can assure you we are treating it as a national security matter."

We know now that the RCMP never found a connection between the Peterborough firearms theft and the convoy protests. Mendicino and Thomas did not know that when they participated in the decision to invoke the Emergencies Act. They went into the meeting with reason to believe things were spiralling out of control across the country.

* * *

It's funny how often decision-making becomes a funnel and no matter how hard you try to punch out the walls of the funnel, everything narrows to the thing you were always going to do.

David Lametti testified that the Emergencies Act had been on every minister's mind since the first days of the COVID-19 pandemic. How could it not have been? All through 2020 and 2021, every time two provinces responded to the virus in different ways, a diversity of approach that should have been a strength of federalism in a new situation, a reporter would ask Trudeau whether he was going to dust off the Emergencies Act to impose a uniform response.

It's hardly surprising that as early as January 30, when everybody in Ottawa began to realize the weekend's trucks weren't leaving, Lametti emailed his chief of staff and asked whether the Emergencies Act might be employed. That email, coming a few days into the crisis, was what made Lametti repeat five times in ninety seconds that he was being "prudent."

The walls narrowed. On February 3, the Cabinet Committee on Safety, Security and Emergencies, a standing committee with no decision-making power, considered the convoy occupation. The various options for federal engagement in the situation were distilled into a single-page chart the officials called a "placemat." At this point, the feds hadn't had much chance to work themselves into a frenzy over all the things the convoy occupiers might do, so the placemat doesn't even mention the Emergencies Act. There is instead a lot of talk about aid the feds might provide to the City of Ottawa and to the provinces. There's also one lonely box labelled "Engagement With Protesters." Who would even talk to these heathen? Should a cabinet minister get the assignment? A public servant? A private citizen sent as an emissary? Who would that person be?

On the other side of the placemat, under "Creative Alternatives," some brave soul noted that after the 2019 Yellow Vest protests in France, the government launched a "national listening exercise." Emmanuel Macron had even attended some of the meetings.

At 8 a.m. on February 9, after another heavy weekend of protests (the weekends were always worse as people drove in from out of town to swell temporarily the ranks of the convoy), Janice Charette chaired a meeting of deputy ministers. "My intention was to try to say to my deputy minister colleagues, 'We have to leave no stone unturned. We have to make sure that we are looking at every power, duty, every authority we have, every resource we have to make sure we are bringing the full power of the federal government and its resources to try to help those who are frontline responsibility.'"

No stone unturned? "All hands on deck," she added. "No idea too crazy. Let's look at absolutely everything."

Rob Stewart was at that meeting. As deputy minister of Public Safety, he was Marco Mendicino's civil-service lieutenant. Stewart is a University of Ottawa MBA who spent sixteen years at the Department of Finance before being asked to run Public Safety, a department where he'd never worked, four months before the COVID lockdown began. His testimony to Rouleau suggested a lively intelligence, an independent mind, and limited familiarity with the files he suddenly had to juggle.

As one might in such circumstances, Stewart kept a close eye on the politicians for social cues. At a February 7 meeting of federal and provincial public-safety deputy ministers, Stewart had told his colleagues about the situation in Ottawa. There was "no degree of violent extremism going on," he said, but there sure was a lot of frustration: "In Ottawa, the law has been disregarded. The norms of behaviour and laws."

The last line in the summary of Stewart's remarks to the provincial ministers was: "Strong desire to not engage protesters and to let enforcement take its course." What did that mean? Said Stewart: "That last line refers to essentially the decision by ministers not to speak to the protesters."

As a public servant, Rob Stewart was not supposed to have strong opinions about the government. But he kept thinking for himself and learning in his new role. After all, Janice Charette had told deputy ministers no idea was too crazy. So on February 10, Stewart briefed the cabinet's Incident Response Group about a chat he'd had that very morning with Marcel Beaudin, the head of the OPP's Provincial Liaison Team. "The negotiator suggested that the leaders of the protest could potentially be encouraged to leave and denounce the blockade in exchange for a commitment to register their message with the government."

Given the government's "strong desire to not engage," these were cheeky thoughts to entertain. But smart people, including Brenda Lucki, had told Stewart to talk to Beaudin. So Stewart heard him out on this notion of give and take, win-win, de-escalation. "It was very educational for me," he testified. Beaudin said if some of the convoy leaders—well, leaders "of a sort"—could find someone important to talk to, "this would have the effect of allowing people to achieve something," Stewart said. And they might go home. Not all of them, of course. But the intensive police action that would follow would at least face a smaller crowd of holdouts.

"So the intention would have been . . ." Shantona Chaudhury began.

Stewart finished her thought: "Shrink it."

So here was Stewart, caught between what his government didn't want and what his police contacts said might work. Inevitably, he got squeezed. It didn't take long. On February 11, a day after Stewart briefed the IRG, Mendicino learned that Stewart had drafted a plan to have Ontario and federal officials talk to the protesters, as City of Ottawa officials and any number of cops had already been doing.

This notion of talking to the protesters, rather than letting Jim Watson and the saps down at Ottawa City Hall talk to them, was always dependent on ministerial approval. Mendicino most certainly did not approve. He texted Katie Telford, Trudeau's chief of staff, to let her know he had headed off Stewart's display of heterodoxy. "Very last minute (and thin)," he said of his deputy's work. "Flagging as a concern and inconsistent with good info flow. . . . Sorry—but had to let you know."

The strong desire to not engage won. Mendicino shut Stewart down on February 11. The walls of the funnel constricted to a single option. On Sunday, the IRG met without input from RCMP Commissioner Brenda Lucki, apart from the false alarm about the Peterborough firearm theft. On Monday, Trudeau had a conference call with the premiers. Most told him not to use the Emergencies Act. Ontario's Doug Ford, who had kept his ministers from meeting with the feds and the City of Ottawa about managing the crisis and who ignored a summons from Rouleau's commission counsel to explain his choices, was a big fan of the Emergencies Act. The law requires consultation but not support. The premiers could have been unanimous in opposing the use of the act and Trudeau would still have been able to invoke it. In the end, it wasn't unanimous.

In his testimony on Rouleau's last day of hearings, Trudeau was asked what it felt like to sign the memo from Janice Charette recommending the use of the act.

"I reflected briefly on, first of all, the reassurance that it gave me that all the inputs in the system had come up to the [privy council] clerk," he said. As the clerk and Jody Thomas and others had testified, all the inputs in the system had not in fact come up to the clerk.

"I also reflected on, 'OK, what if I don't sign it? . . . What if I decided, 'You know what? Let's give it a few days'?"

He worried about whether "the worst" would have happened in those few days. "What if someone had gotten hurt? What if a police officer had been put in the hospital? . . . I would have worn that in a way that we would certainly be talking about, in a forum such as this."

On its face, the prime minister's implied test for invocation of the Emergencies Act was whether or not it would keep a hypothetical cop out of a hypothetical hospital, which is nearly the lowest imaginable bar. Three months after Trudeau testified, Rouleau would be generous in setting a much higher bar and announcing that Trudeau had cleared it.

Trudeau's is not the last word, nor even Rouleau's. The Emergencies Act does not strip any Canadian of their Charter rights and several legal challenges to the act on Charter grounds proceed. The judges who consider those challenges will take Rouleau into account, but his report doesn't bind them.

There is no need to speculate about the effect this first use of the Emergencies Act will have on the way Canadians are governed for years to come. It's not a hypothetical question. We are all going to find out.

On February 21, 2022, two days before his government officially withdrew the Emergencies Act, Justin Trudeau gave a news conference with four senior cabinet ministers. He seemed to be trying to strike a different tone.

"There's a lesson for all of us in what happened this month. We don't know when this pandemic is going to finally end, but that doesn't mean we can't start healing as a nation. And it starts with all of us. If you spend a lot of time online, try looking outside your social media bubble every now and then. If you have a cousin who you haven't seen in a while because they're unvaccinated or because they're vaccinated, give them a call. If a political conversation got heated during a recent gathering and a friend or relative left early, pick up the phone. Not to try to convince them, not to argue, but simply to ask how they're doing."

Stay in Ottawa long enough and you get used to politicians demanding more civility from *other* people. Was I too optimistic to think I heard some introspection from this one? "Look, in the heat of the moment, we can all get carried away trying to win an argument. But not every single conversation has to be about winning an argument."

I could have filled this book with arguments about the central legal dispute of the Emergencies Act debate, which was whether the convoy met the act's definition of a threat to national security. It's a good question. It has a mystery at its centre, because Trudeau and his attorney general David Lametti refused to waive solicitor-client privilege, so we can't know how they justified their decision, even to themselves. But I decided to leave the question of the act's legal threshold to others because I'm not sure it's the most important question.

I think the important question is whether we hear one another. Even when we're tired. Even when we're scared.

RESPONSE TO SUTHERLAND QUARTERLY ISSUE 1, 2022

By Kenneth Whyte

In each edition of *Sutherland Quarterly*, we include responses to the previous book, in this instance John Fraser's *Funeral for a Queen: Twelve Days in London*. As publisher of the series, I do not intend to weigh in on each book we release but Fraser made me a character in *Funeral for a Queen* and all but begged for an answer.

I had written a newsletter, after Queen Elizabeth died and before Fraser wrote his book, detailing King Charles behaviour in his first public acts (https://shush.substack.com/p/all-hail-king-eeyore). I deemed this behaviour significant because Charles had been waiting impatiently his whole seventy-three-years to perform these acts and had plenty of time to prepare and contemplate the impression he would make on his subjects. Also, he'd made it clear over the years that he believed he could out-shine his late mother in this whole monarchy business.

Yet in his first public performance he repeatedly flashed pettiness, irritation, and selfishness in full view of television cameras that he knew to be rolling. This pettifoggery peaked when the fresh king got ink on his fingers while signing official papers:

"Oh god, I hate this (pen)!" Charles said to Queen Consort Camilla as he stood up, handing her the offending instrument.

"Oh look, it's going everywhere," said Camilla as Charles wiped his fingers.

"I can't bear this bloody thing," he continued, walking away. "Every stinking time."

I found it especially amusing that while fuming over the performance of a writing instrument before a global audience, Charles' first impulse was to hand the "bloody thing" to Camilla so it could leak on her hands. It made me wonder what kind of king we'd be singing for God to save.

For this Fraser accused me of "pop-psychological potshot analysis" and a slur on "the most resilient and decent public figure currently on the go."

I could quarrel with "pop-psychological," because I was observing, not interpreting. I could quarrel with "resilient," unless Fraser simply meant old, which is indisputable. And I could quarrel with "decent" because what decent man stained by a disloyal pen would insist his wife suffer the same indignity?

I choose instead to admire the agility with which Fraser side-stepped the abundant evidence I presented to demonstrate that King Charles' performance at his signing-in, or whatever it's called, was of a piece with a lifetime of questionable behavior, starting with his spotty record in the armed forces and the dedication of his twenties and thirties to polo and test-driving other men's wives, on through to his messy marriage and bungled divorce and one of the most embarrassing personal scandals (tampongate) in the modern history of the monarchy (which is saying something). Not to mention his record as "a hopeless executive" in the running of his personal office with its officially documented "litany of sloppy-record-keeping, law administration, and bureaucratic foul-ups," the revelation of which led his own father to conclude he was not up to the top job in the House of Windsor. Or his acceptance of "donations" to his private charities from a Russian convict, a Taiwanese fugitive, a Saudi businessman who later received honours from the Crown, and the prime minister of Quatar who packed €3 million cash into suitcases and carrier bags and handed it over at meetings not recorded on the court circular. Or his need for five homes and a personal staff of ninety (compared to his equally active father's staff of four), including a valet to squeeze his toothpaste and iron his shoelaces and pack the toilet seat and teddy bear this resilient and decent man never travels without. Or his constant whining about his lot in life, a habit enthusiastically adopted by his second-born, Prince Harry, who devoted almost the whole of his recently released memoir to its exercise.

Sweep these details aside and Charles indeed can appear ready, as Fraser writes, "to show the world that he can make good on his solemn oath of service." One can almost see him as "wise" and "dutiful," his doubters as "churlish," and come to believe that he "won't disappoint."

Fraser emphasizes the king's embrace of the causes of global warming and Indigenous reconciliation as evidence of a long head, reasons to trust his competence and modernity. And it may be that Charles has a sincere and well-considered attachment to these causes and that they are not more evidence of the intellectual faddishness that led him to embrace coffee enemas as a cure for cancer. He has put real effort into Indigenous relations and has made a small start—or at least talked of making a small start—on reducing a family carbon footprint that would make a tech titan blush.

Charles deserves some credit for his early moves as King. He kicked his reprehensible brother, Andrew, out of Royal Lodge, his luxurious thirty-room crib in Windsor Park. He also reclaimed Frogmore Cottage, which his mother had gifted to Harry and Meghan on the occasion of their wedding. The ingrate Sussexes didn't deserve to keep it.

I still don't think we have cause to expect much of Charles' reign. But I sincerely hope Fraser's optimism is not misplaced, largely for the sake of his mother, whose legacy the author justly celebrates in *Funeral for a Queen*. She deserves a competent successor and appears to have done her best to leave one. We'll see.

---

by Andrew Cohen

From before the age of nine, John Fraser has been besotted with the British monarchy. Since he was introduced to its splendour by his Glaswegian grandmother before the coronation of Queen Elizabeth

II in 1953, the institution has beguiled him. As the Empire dissolved, Great Britain declined and the family turned dysfunctional, Canada's "royal romantic" has remained spellbound.

Today, the monarchy for Fraser is a secular evangelism whose magic no one with a shilling of wonder can resist. "I feel sorry for those who don't get it," he laments of the Great Unmoved. "It must be like people who think opera is all about the plot and the music is merely incidental."

(As he notes in his pages, my take on the monarchy is "negative indifference." John has been my editor, mentor and friend of some 35 years. He is generous, impish and witty, an adornment to public life as journalist, author, advocate and educator–his royalism notwithstanding).

Funeral for the Queen: Twelve Days in London recounts the period from the death of Queen Elizabeth II to the accession of her heir, King Charles III. It is a valentine to the institution. Deeply personal, sometimes funny, every well-crafted passage radiates a boyish exuberance, as if drawn from *Arabian Nights*. Then again, what would we expect from the founding president of the Institute for the Study of the Monarchy in Canada?

A mutual friend thinks this is the book Fraser was meant to write. In a lifetime of service to the Crown, this panegyric is his crowning achievement.

As devout royal subject, with no claim to objectivity, Fraser is a reliable reporter. He leaves no ritual, rite or custom—however ancient or obscure—unmentioned or uncelebrated. We learn, in particular, of Fraser's personal mission to London, delivering sacred tobacco from Indigenous lands to the chief Chapel Royal at St. James's Palace. And his conversation with the Queen and her oblique reference to the "very great tragedy" of King Edward VIII, which haunts him still.

All this Fraser conveys with charm. He is in his milieu, after all, and he cannot understand how anyone else does not share his royal fascination. Indeed, to think otherwise is a form of lèse-majesté. Gleefully he rounds on the faithless.

Hilary Mantel is a "know-it-all." Scottish First Minister Nicola Sturgeon is "an almost embarrassing bit player in the funeral of the century" and "a feisty bundle of worked up independence and curious insecurity." No doubt his scorn sent Sturgeon into therapy prompted her recent resignation. Lesser republicans are "mainly middle-aged men, facing constipation, looming incontinence or merely lack of imagination." On Edward's anti-Semitism and Nazi sympathies, allegations of racism in the royal family or its long-running melodrama of divorce, desertion and misbehaviour, Fraser is largely silent.

Oh, the agony of the unenamoured. *Those who don't get it.* Alas, in the contemporary world, it is Fraser, bless him, who doesn't get it.

What he doesn't get is why Canadians, and other peoples of the realm, see the monarchy with indifference today. Diverting, perhaps, but unimportant to their lives. Whatever their personal affection for Elizabeth and respect for her extraordinary service, the institution is an anachronism.

Monarchists love to trumpet the King's affection for Canada, but it isn't enough in a country with a founding francophone minority and a growing diversity, rooted in places with an unhappy colonial past. However, the monarchy is sown into Canada, historically, symbolically and constitutionally, the monarch remains a foreigner. And why, pray tell, would a sophisticated, modern people want to be represented by someone who lives in London?

Others have made up their minds. India dissolved its ties with the monarchy long ago. More recently, so has Barbados. Jamaica, New Zealand and Australia may follow. They are among the fourteen countries that retain the British monarchy as a colonial relic.

Canada, for our part, has been distancing itself from Great Britain for a century. Step by step, we have been asserting ourselves: creating the Canadian Corps (1915); assuming direct responsibility for foreign relations (1931); establishing national citizenship (1947); making the Supreme Court of Canada (not the British Privy Council), the final arbiter (1949); appointing the first native-born Canadian governor general (1952); adopting the Maple Leaf as national flag (1965).

Our foremost decision was patriating the British North America Act and entrenching the Charter of Rights and Freedoms (1982). For Pierre Elliott Trudeau, this was the single greatest act of statesmanship in our history. It freed our founding document from British trusteeship and presaged the last, logical step in our march to maturity: becoming a republic.

This is a debate we long avoided, either out of lassitude or politeness to Queen Elizabeth. It is one we owe ourselves now. (Even Fraser, much annoyed by our government's indifference to the coronation of King Charles in May, thinks we should have *the* conversation.)

He and others argue that dissolving our ties to the monarchy would require reopening the constitution, which is messy, and winning consent from all ten provinces, which is improbable. Which is why the royalists can relax. The break won't happen imminently because we are uninterested, as we are so many things that would make us a fuller country: adopting a form of proportional representation, abolishing the Senate, developing a true economic union, returning seriously to the world. Or embracing great national projects, such as building high-speed rail.

What we can do, though, is detach ourselves from the monarchy. Refuse to put Charles on coins, bills and postage stamps. Remove "royal" from our navy and air force and other institutions. Discourage royal visits. And play down the coronation, much as we decently can.

Without the will or the way to become a republic, the future of contented Canada is monarchy lite—an institution that survives with a shallow footprint. Unheard, unseen and ignored, the disappearing Crown would reflect our exquisite ambiguity, annoying republicans and royalists alike while allowing us to muddle through, as always. How perfectly Canadian.

Andrew Cohen is a journalist, professor of journalism at Carleton University and the author of *The Unfinished Canadian: The People We Are*. He is founding president of The Historica-Dominion Institute (Historica Canada).

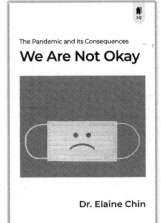

GET THE <u>WHOLE</u> STORY

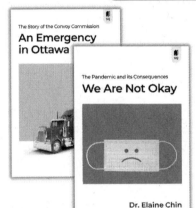